Set design by David P. Gordon

Photo by Alan Kolc

The set from the Arden Theatre Company and The People's Light and Theatre Company production of *Tiny Island.*

TINY ISLAND

BY MICHAEL HOLLINGER

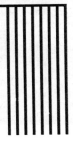

DRAMATISTS
PLAY SERVICE
INC.

SPECIAL NOTE
Anyone receiving permission to produce TINY ISLAND is required to give credit to the Author as sole and exclusive Author of the Play on the title page of all programs distributed in connection with performances of the Play and in all instances in which the title of the Play appears for purposes of advertising, publicizing or otherwise exploiting the Play and/or a production thereof. The name of the Author must appear on a separate line, in which no other name appears, immediately beneath the title and in size of type equal to 50% of the size of the largest, most prominent letter used for the title of the Play. No person, firm or entity may receive credit larger or more prominent than that accorded the Author. The following acknowledgment must appear on the title page in all programs distributed in connection with performances of the Play:

TINY ISLAND was originally produced by Arden Theatre Company,
Philadelphia, Pennsylvania and The People's Light and Theatre Company,
Malvern, Pennsylvania. It was written under a Playwright Fellowship from
Pennsylvania Council on the Arts, received a Roger L. Stevens Award
from the Fund for New American Plays, and was workshopped at
the Guthrie Theater as part of a Pew Playwright Exchange.

For Ann Hollinger and Margie Bellwoar,
and the little girls inside you.

ACKNOWLEDGMENTS

For developmental readings and workshops, thanks to: Seth Rozin and the Philadelphia Art Alliance; Sara Garonzik, the late Adrienne Neye, and Philadelphia Theatre Company; Elizabeth Dowd and Bloomsburg Theatre Ensemble; Nancy Borgenicht, Al Nevins, and Salt Lake Acting Company; Stephen DiMenna, Michael Lupu, and the Guthrie Theater; Elissa Adams and The Playwrights' Center; Doug Bauer and the Pew Charitable Trusts; and the many talented actors who wrestled with the play and helped render its characters 3-D. For insight: Harriet Power, David Callaghan, Ellen Metz, Milton Shils, and Megan Bellwoar. For financial support: Mrs. Carole Haas, the 1996 F. Otto Haas Award Committee, and the Pennsylvania Council on the Arts. For professional guidance: Mary Harden and Harden-Curtis Associates. For their continuing commitment to my work, and their tireless devotion to getting it right: Terry Nolen and Arden Theatre Company. Thank you all.

TINY ISLAND was originally produced by Arden Theatre Company (Aaron Posner, Artistic Director; Terrence J. Nolen, Producing Artistic Director; Amy Murphy, Managing Director) in Philadelphia, Pennsylvania, and The People's Light and Theatre Company (Abigail Adams, Artistic Director; Stephen Novelli, Associate Artistic Director; Grace E. Grillet, General Manager) in Malvern, Pennsylvania. The co-production opened in Philadelphia on November 20, 1997 and opened in Malvern on January 14, 1998. It was directed by Terrence J. Nolen; the set design was by David P. Gordon; the lighting design was by Martha Mountain; the sound design was by Bob Perdick; the costume design was by Ramona Broomer; and the production stage managers were Debi Marcucci (Arden) and Peter Wrenn-Meleck (People's Light). The cast was as follows:

MURIEL .... Carla Belver
HAZEL .... Alda Cortese
MIKE/NORM .... Kevin O'Donnell
YOUNG MURIEL/BRENDA .... Suli Holum

TINY ISLAND was written under a Playwright Fellowship from Pennsylvania Council on the Arts and received a 1995 Roger L. Stevens Award from the Fund for New American Plays, a project of the John F. Kennedy Center for the Performing Arts with support from American Express Company in cooperation with the President's Committee on the Arts and Humanities. It was work-shopped at the Guthrie Theater in Minneapolis as part of a Pew Playwright Exchange.

CHARACTERS

TINY ISLAND requires four actors to play six roles:

MURIEL — Late forties.
HAZEL — Early fifties. Sister to Muriel.
MIKE — Seventeen. Boyfriend to Brenda. (Doubles with Norm.)
NORM — Seventeen. (Played by the actor playing Mike.)
YOUNG MURIEL — Seventeen. (Doubles with Brenda.)
BRENDA — Seventeen. Girlfriend to Mike. (Played by the actress playing Young Muriel.)

PLACE

The projection booth of the Brynwyd Classic Cinema, located in an affluent suburb on Philadelphia's Main Line.

TIME

Early 1980s.

SYNOPSIS OF SCENES

ACT ONE
Reel One: a weekend night in February.
Reel Two: another weekend night in February.
Reel Three: the night after Reel One.

CHANGEOVER

ACT TWO
Reel Four: late afternoon, three days later.
Reel Five: later that evening.

NOTE

When one character begins speaking before the other has finished, the point of interruption is marked /.

TINY ISLAND

ACT ONE

Reel One

In darkness, the voices of two little girls playing. Though the specific words may be difficult to discern, their hushed, reverent tone indicates that this is a game of significance. The voices echo slightly at first, then gradually more so, until by the end they create a haunting effect.

GIRL #1. *(V.O.)* Pilot to navigator, come in navigator.
GIRL #2. *(V.O.)* Navigator here.
GIRL #1. *(V.O.)* Prepare for night flight. *(Beat.)* All electric power off, radio off.
GIRL #2. *(V.O.)* All electric power off, radio off.
GIRL #1. *(V.O.)* All controls adjusted and trimmed.
GIRL #2. *(V.O.)* Check. Ailerons normal position.
GIRL #1. *(V.O.)* Check. Elevators normal position.
GIRL #2. *(V.O.)* Check.
GIRL #1. *(V.O.)* Prime engines.
GIRL #2. *(V.O.)* Number one and number two mixture rich.
GIRL #1. *(V.O.)* Crank engine one.
GIRL #2. *(V.O.)* Engine one cranked.
GIRL #1. *(V.O.)* Crank engine two.
GIRL #2. *(V.O.)* Engine two cranked.
GIRL #1. *(V.O.)* Advance down runway ... *(Voices echo eerily as lights come up on the projection booth of an old movie theater. It has*

9

*one visible entrance from a stairway, as well as a door leading into a
small adjoining bathroom. This is not a tidy place; everything seems to
be covered by a layer of dust from the Golden Age of Cinema; walls are
dominated by large old movie posters, broken up by an occasional calendar or Chinese restaurant menu. In fact, the walls may be entirely
established by these items, with large gaps through which we see only
the darkness beyond. There is a cracked mirror, a wall phone, a high
stool, two chairs, and a table upon which sit film reels, splicing
equipment, notebooks, etc. Most prominent in the room are two old
movie projectors, both facing the audience. The L projector is rolling,
its light shining out into the darkness. From a distance, a young man's
voice is heard calling:)*
MIKE. *(Off.)* Um, excuse me … *(Beat. Muriel Palmer, a woman
in her late forties appears in the doorway, slightly winded from the
stairs. Upon entering she is immediately struck by the memory of the
place, and moves gradually into the room, taking it in.)* Hello? *(Beat.
The voice gets closer:)* Excuse me … *(After a moment, Mike, a sev-
enteen-year-old movie usher in regulation bow tie and red jacket,
appears in the doorway, also somewhat winded. He stops upon seeing
Muriel, who seems not to notice him as she studies the space she stands
in.)* See, I told you she wasn't up here. *(Beat.)* She said she was
going out for cigarettes, but she'd be back for the changeover, so.
(Pause.) So she'll be back really soon. *(Muriel turns to look at him.)*
MURIEL. Oh. Good. *(Muriel examines a photograph which has been
thumbtacked to one of the walls. Mike quickly checks the stairway.)*
MIKE. Um … does she know you?
MURIEL. *(Beat.)* Hmm?
MIKE. Mrs. Breen know you?
MURIEL. *(Half to herself.)* Oh yeah.
MIKE. Are you, like, friends?
MURIEL. Not much like friends, no. Not anymore. *(Muriel
crosses to the moving projector and looks at it in fascination.)*
MIKE. If you want to go back down, I'll tell her you're here.
MURIEL. That's okay.
MIKE. When she gets back.
MURIEL. I'll wait.
MIKE. *(Beat.)* 'Cause there's really not supposed to be anybody
up here except her. *(Muriel looks at him.)*

MURIEL. You're up here.

MIKE. Yeah, well. She lets me. You know, hang out and talk, or play Trivial Pursuit, or whatever.

MURIEL. You're, like, friends.

MIKE. I guess. *(Muriel nods vaguely and continues looking around. Pause. Mike watches her carefully.)* You know her from school?

MURIEL. Hmm?

MIKE. You two go to college together?

MURIEL. Oh. No, I never went. *(She looks back at the projector. Pause.)*

MIKE. I'm going to La Salle next fall. "Class of '87." My girl-friend got into UMass *and* La Salle, but I think she should go to La Salle. You know, stick around. *(Muriel reaches out a hand to open a panel on the projector.)* I wouldn't touch that. *(Muriel looks at him.)* She doesn't let anybody touch the projector but her.

MURIEL. Except you.

MIKE. Not even me. She doesn't like people messing with her stuff.

MURIEL. Oh, I know. *(Muriel walks D. and looks out a viewport. Mike checks the stairway again.)*

MIKE. So. How do you know Mrs. Breen?

MURIEL. She ... we used to work here.

MIKE. You were a projectionist?

MURIEL. *(Looking out.)* Oh, no. Mr. Brubaker wouldn't let girls be projectionists. Though we certainly spent a lot of time up here. Of course, that was centuries ago. Back before disco and indoor plumbing. *(Beat.)* You ever seen this one before? *(Mike approaches the viewport and looks out.)*

MIKE. What is it?

MURIEL. *My Forbidden Past.* Robert Mitchum and Ava Gardner.

MIKE. No. *(Muriel looks around at the theater through the viewport.)*

MURIEL. You should've seen this place in its heyday. With the brass shined up, red velour draped everywhere ... Like a palace. We used to go around once a week and brush the seats.

MIKE. You brushed the seats?

MURIEL. Every Saturday night.

MIKE. Huh.

MURIEL. Then we filled them all for *The Bad and the Beautiful* or ... *Singin' in the Rain* ... or *Wings Over Water.* Hardly anybody

11

I knew had a boob tube yet; we thought it was just a fad.

MIKE. "Boob tube"?

MURIEL. Idiot box, TV. *(Beat.)* You ever seen *Wings Over Water?*

MIKE. Is that the lady who swims all the time?

MURIEL. *(Beat.)* You mean Esther Williams?

MIKE. Yeah!

MURIEL. No.

MIKE. Oh. It sounded kinda familiar.

MURIEL. It should. It's on the schedule for tomorrow.

MIKE. *That's* how I heard of it. Isn't that the one with what's-his-name in it?

MURIEL. Philip Archer.

MIKE. No, that guy from *My Three Sons.*

MURIEL. Oh. Yeah, he's in there too. *(Muriel looks out the view-port again.)*

MIKE. I thought it sounded familiar. We showed a bunch with that swimmer lady last month, but they all look the same to me.

MURIEL. *(Quietly.)* "I've loved you to the stars, I'll love you to the bottom of the sea."

MIKE. Huh?

MURIEL. Lord knows why they made it in 3-D. It's not like it's *Creature from the Black Lagoon* ... I guess it was just the hot new thing.

MIKE. What is it, like a love story?

MURIEL. Oh yeah. Love, honor, adventure ... And who could forget Philip Archer in his flying togs and leather helmet, kissing Charlotte Ayres as the sun comes up ... *(Muriel's eyes have begun to well up.)* "I love you." "Oh, do you really mean it?" "I've loved you to the stars, I'll love you to the bottom of the sea." *(She is deeply affected by the memory. Pause. Suddenly, a light, clear bell begins ringing, about once per second. Muriel is shaken from her reverie.)* Holy moley ...

MIKE. Huh?

MURIEL. What's that? *(Muriel, a bit frightened, gives her head a quick, slight shake.)*

MIKE. What.

MURIEL. *Tell me you hear it.*

MIKE. You mean the changeover bell?

MURIEL. What *is* that?

MIKE. On the projector. Wakes you up when the changeover's coming.

MURIEL. Change...?

MIKE. You know, in case you're asleep.

MURIEL. Oh ... right. *(Muriel begins fanning herself.)*

MIKE. You okay?

MURIEL. Um ... yeah.

MIKE. You look like you just seen a ghost or something.

MURIEL. I ... just haven't been up here in a long time.

MIKE. Pretty different?

MURIEL. *(Looking around.)* Not a bit. It's exactly the same.

MIKE. I can believe that. Look, you can even write your name in the dust. *(Mike writes his name in the dust. Muriel watches him, shaken by the image.)*

MURIEL. Um ... Can I use the bathroom?

MIKE. I guess she won't mind. *(Muriel starts toward the bathroom.)* Don't forget to jiggle.

MURIEL. Huh?

MIKE. The handle. *(He demonstrates.)* It leaks. *(Muriel nods vaguely and exits into the bathroom. Mike sits at the table, rolls a die, looks; rolls again, looks; rolls again, looks, and finally moves a piece on a game board. Hazel Breen appears in the doorway, slightly winded. Though she is probably only in her early fifties, she is dressed carelessly and looks rather the worse for wear.)*

HAZEL. Whoever designed those stairs didn't smoke.

MIKE. Hey.

HAZEL. Hey yourself.

MIKE. Changeover's coming.

HAZEL. Bell ring yet?

MIKE. Yeah, just.

HAZEL. Did Ray call?

MIKE. No.

HAZEL. *(Half to herself.)* Son of a bitch ... *(She looks at her watch, then checks the remaining film on the reel.)*

MIKE. There's a lady in the bathroom.

HAZEL. My bathroom?

MIKE. Said she's taking Brenda's place in concessions.

13

HAZEL. *(Half to herself.)* The Old Man tells me nothing ... You tell her she wasn't allowed up here?

MIKE. Yeah, but she wouldn't go back down. Said she knows you.

HAZEL. *(Beat. Baffled:)* Huh. *(Hazel looks out the viewport for a few seconds, then pushes a button on the side of the projector. Instantly, that projector's light goes out and the R projector comes on. Hazel crosses to the game board.)* Did you roll?

MIKE. Yeah.

HAZEL. What'd you get?

MIKE. Pink.

HAZEL. Liar. What'd you really get?

MIKE. Pink.

HAZEL. You're so full of shit.

MIKE. I did.

HAZEL. How come you land on pink every time I leave the room?

MIKE. Lucky, I guess.

HAZEL. Roll again.

MIKE. I landed on pink!

HAZEL. *(Handing him the dice.)* Roll.

MIKE. Aw, man ... *(He rolls.)*

HAZEL. Yellow, that's more like it. *(Hazel pulls out a question card from the box.)*

MIKE. I suck at History.

HAZEL. Tough. *(Reading.)* "Who was the first aviatrix to fly solo across the Atlantic Ocean?"

MIKE. *(Beat.)* The first what? *(The bathroom door opens. Hearing it, Hazel turns and sees Muriel standing in the doorway.)*

HAZEL. Oh, Jesus Christ.

MURIEL. Hi, Hazel.

HAZEL. Jesus Christ. *(Pause.)*

MURIEL. Is that all you can say?

HAZEL. *(Beat.)* I think so. Jesus. What are you doing here?

MURIEL. Daddy didn't tell you I was here? *(Beat. Hazel chuckles softly and shakes her head in disbelief.)*

HAZEL. You know the Old Man ...

MURIEL. Well ... I just got in a few hours ago. Aunt Esther called me about the heart attack —

HAZEL. Well he won't have a bypass, won't take his medicine,

14

what do you expect?

MURIEL. Apparently this one was worse than the others.

HAZEL. It wasn't pretty. I'd say you got here just in time.

MURIEL. *(Beat.)* He's not that bad, is he?

HAZEL. I meant, to avoid the mess.

MURIEL. Oh. I would've come sooner, but I had to drop Katie off at Notre Dame yesterday. So, since I was in the neighborhood …

HAZEL. Indiana being in the neighborhood …

MURIEL. Well, it is when you live in Texas. *(Beat.)* Anyway, here I am.

HAZEL. Here you are. *(Beat. To Mike:)* Whose roll?

MURIEL. You look good.

HAZEL. No I don't.

MURIEL. *(Beat.)* No, you don't.

HAZEL. I wish I could blame it all on my barber, but he's not responsible for the wear and tear. Did you jiggle?

MURIEL. Excuse me? *(Hazel demonstrates, deliberately.)* Oh; yeah.

HAZEL. Then I guess you're all done up here.

MURIEL. *(Beat.)* I was hoping we'd have a chance to talk.

HAZEL. Yeah, well I'm in the middle of a very important trivia game here. *(To Mike.)* Roll.

MURIEL. Can it wait?

HAZEL. Trivia waits for no man, Muriel; it just keeps piling up when you're not looking.

MIKE. I can go if you want.

MURIEL. Thank you.

HAZEL. No, let's play.

MIKE. *(Standing.)* Really, it's no problem.

HAZEL. Sit. *(Mike sits. Pause.)*

MURIEL. Daddy did tell me you and Ray got divorced. *(Pause.)*

HAZEL. Did he.

MURIEL. I'm sorry.

HAZEL. We're not divorced; we're separated.

MURIEL. Oh. Daddy said —

HAZEL. Hey Mike, get me some matches, will you?

MIKE. You got a pack right there.

HAZEL. Well go get me some more. I may want to burn this dump down later, collect the insurance. *(Hazel lights a cigarette.*

Mike exits.) You think the Old Man's got fire insurance?
MURIEL. I ... don't know.
HAZEL. He'd never tell us if he did. Anyway, why bring it up?
MURIEL. I didn't bring it up; *you* —
HAZEL. I mean me and Ray.
MURIEL. Oh. I guess I'm just ... sorry, that's all.
HAZEL. Well. Me too. *(Hazel removes the reel from Projector #1, carries it to the splicing table, and begins removing the splices to separate it into three smaller reels.)* Not that I haven't *asked* for a divorce, but he won't give it to me uncontested. That's the problem with divorces. By the time you need one, you're not on the best of terms with the person you want it from.
MURIEL. Can I ask how it happened?
HAZEL. No. So — how long do you plan to be up here?
MURIEL. Just a couple minutes. I need to keep an eye on the counter.
HAZEL. I meant in Philly.
MURIEL. Oh, just a couple days. Daddy told me his concessions girl just left to work in that video store across the street, so I ... I said I'd fill in while I was here.
HAZEL. What about Norm?
MURIEL. Norm?
HAZEL. Balding? Little dimple?
MURIEL. He ... couldn't come.
HAZEL. You mean he let you go somewhere by yourself?
MURIEL. He had some cable thing in Denver — you know, work work work. *(Hazel resumes work, stops to check her watch, shakes her head in exasperation, then continues working. After a moment:)* Since when has Daddy let you run the projectors?
HAZEL. Since his other guy retired and I needed the cash.
MURIEL. Could you show me how?
HAZEL. Why?
MURIEL. I ... just always wanted to learn.
HAZEL. Well, I always wanted to dance with Elvis, but at some point you realize it's just too late.
MURIEL. It wouldn't have to be tonight ...
HAZEL. Are you listening, Muriel? It's just. Too. Late. Look, I don't mean to be rude, but I'm expecting an important call from a

man I used to love. Anyway, don't you have to go down and sell Jujyfruits or something?

MURIEL. If you want me to leave, just say so.

HAZEL. Leave.

MURIEL. I'm only trying to be civil;

HAZEL. Please leave.

MURIEL. thought after *thirty years* of this nonsense, maybe we could be friends.

HAZEL. And I thought crossing paths every five would fulfill our sisterly obligations. *(They stare at each other for an awkward moment, then Mike appears in the doorway.)*

MIKE. Mrs. Palmer?

MURIEL. *(Beat.)* What?

MIKE. Somebody wants popcorn.

MURIEL. Well ... do you think you could just ... sell them some?

MIKE. I'm an usher.

MURIEL. I know that.

MIKE. Ushers don't sell popcorn.

MURIEL. I thought maybe this one could.

MIKE. We're not supposed to. *(Muriel looks at him a moment, then turns to Hazel.)*

MURIEL. Excuse me. *(She exits. Mike looks after her.)*

HAZEL. *(Half to herself.)* "Of all the gin joints in all the towns in all the world, she walks into mine ... "

MIKE. She never told me she was your sister.

HAZEL. Well she was. *(Hazel crosses to a cooler on the floor.)*

MIKE. Mr. Brubaker's back.

HAZEL. I thought the Old Man went home for the night.

MIKE. He did, but he came back to count the money.

HAZEL. Well, that'll get his little heart pumping again. *(Hazel pulls out a can of beer.)*

MIKE. He wanted me to find out if you're still drinking up here.

HAZEL. *(Half to herself.)* Nobody more righteous than a reformed drunk ... What are you going to tell him? *(She opens the can.)*

MIKE. No. Can I have some? *(She passes him the can. He drinks, winces.)* That's good.

HAZEL. No kidding...? *(Hazel takes the can and drinks.)* Tastes like it's already passed through once to me.

MIKE. I thought it's supposed to taste like that.

HAZEL. At four bucks a case, it's pretty much a given. *(She drinks. Mike checks out his hair in the mirror.)* How's the crowd tonight?

MIKE. Not bad.

HAZEL. How bad?

MIKE. Fifteen, twenty?

HAZEL. That stinks.

MIKE. My parents both came.

HAZEL. They into the oldies?

MIKE. Maybe my mom. My dad just came 'cause his VCR's broken. *(Mike turns and looks at Hazel for a moment.)* You and your sister don't look anything like each other.

HAZEL. That's intentional.

MIKE. *(Beat.)* Do you, like, not get along, or —

HAZEL. I don't want to talk about it, Mike, okay?

MIKE. Okay. *(Mike returns to the mirror. Muriel appears in the doorway, breathing a little heavier.)*

MURIEL. You couldn't get a popcorn for your own mother?

MIKE. It's a girl job.

MURIEL. Why is it a girl job?

MIKE. 'Cause it is. Ushering's a guy job, concessions is a girl job.

MURIEL. Thank you for making that clear to me.

HAZEL. Whose turn is it?

MIKE. Mine. *(Hazel hands him the die. Mike rolls.)*

MURIEL. Hazel? *(Hazel ignores her, pulling a question card as Mike moves his game piece.)*

MIKE. Pink.

HAZEL. Son of a bitch. *(She reads the card.)* "What weekly series starred Jerry Van Dyke as — " wait a second, you already went.

MIKE. No, I didn't.

HAZEL. Liar, you landed on yellow.

MIKE. I didn't get to go, though.

HAZEL. *(Moving his game piece.)* You are such a cheat. Where's the card?

MURIEL. Hazel …

MIKE. That's not the yellow I was on.

HAZEL. Here it is: "Who was the first — "

MURIEL. *Mike* ... would you mind if Mrs. Breen and I talked for a bit? *(Hazel looks up.)*
MIKE. No, go ahead. *(He remains seated.)*
MURIEL. I meant ... would you mind getting some matches or cigarettes or whatever it is you get while we talk?
HAZEL. Muriel ...
MIKE. Oh. Okay. *(He stands.)*
HAZEL. Sit down.
MIKE. No, no, that's okay.
MURIEL. Thank you.
MIKE. *(To Hazel.)* No biggie. I'll just hang out downstairs.
MURIEL. I appreciate it. *(He exits. Hazel exhales loudly, shakes her head in exasperation, and returns to her splicing.)* I'm sorry to interrupt your "important" game, but —
HAZEL. No you're not.
MURIEL. You and Mike can play this ... whatchamacallit anytime. *(Pause; Hazel continues working.)* Well you can. *(Hazel slams down a film can.)*
HAZEL. This is a union projection room. You know what that means?
MURIEL. *(Crossing her arms.)* They let you march in the Labor Day parade?
HAZEL. It means if you're not in the union, you're in deep shit for even setting foot up here.
MURIEL. We haven't talked to each other in ages.
HAZEL. Well maybe that's a good thing.
MURIEL. Well maybe it isn't.
HAZEL. Well maybe it is.
MURIEL. Well maybe you — no, this is stupid. Arguing like we're five-year-olds ...
HAZEL. You started it.
MURIEL. *You* star — no, just ... drop it. *(Muriel exhales heavily, frustrated, and fans herself. After a moment:)* Is it hot up here, or is it me? *(Hazel regards her carefully.)*
HAZEL. You. *(Pause.)*
MURIEL. Awful, isn't it — across the street? *(Hazel checks her watch.)* What happened to the dry cleaners?
HAZEL. Papadopoulos bought them out.

19

MURIEL. Papadopoulos? What, the pizza guy?

HAZEL. Now he's trying to expand the video store, but Nolan's won't sell.

MURIEL. I think it's awful. Norm got me a video thing last Christmas, and I have yet to watch it. You don't own one, do you?

HAZEL. Do I look like a woman on the cutting edge? My whole wardrobe is a monument to the Ford Administration.

MURIEL. It's not that bad ...

HAZEL. Oh, please.

MURIEL. It's really the haircut more than the clothes. *(Hazel looks at her.)* Not that there's anything wrong with your hair. It's just not ... I mean it's fine, it's — really. Your hair can do so many things, and this ... this is ... one of them.

HAZEL. Muriel.

MURIEL. What.

HAZEL. Why are you here?

MURIEL. *(Beat.)* I told you, I found out Daddy —

HAZEL. Not in Philly, up here. What do you want from me?

MURIEL. Nothing.

HAZEL. Then get out.

MURIEL. Why are you — ?

HAZEL. If you want something, say it; if you don't, get out.

MURIEL. Why do I have to want something?

HAZEL. Because you and I are talking about haircuts.

MURIEL. I'm sorry I brought up the haircut ...

HAZEL. I don't give a shit about the haircut, I want to know what you want from me.

MURIEL. I don't *want* anything, I just —

HAZEL. *(Walking to the phone.)* All right, then, I'm telling Mike to come up and finish our trivia game ...

MURIEL. Don't do that ...

HAZEL. *(Picking up the receiver.)* Why not?

MURIEL. We never get a chance to talk ...

HAZEL. *(Pushing a button or two.)* And look to what good use we're putting our time.

MURIEL. Wait, just let me —

HAZEL. Hi, Mike?

MURIEL. Hazel ...

20

HAZEL. *(Into phone.)* You want to finish / the game?

MURIEL. I'll tell you *I'll tell you!*

HAZEL. *(To phone.)* Just a second. *(She covers the phone. To Muriel.)* No bullshit?

MURIEL. No b ... No. *(Hazel looks at her a second, then speaks into the phone.)*

HAZEL. Yeah, you want to finish the game tomorrow? *(Beat.)* The hell you did, we only — *(Beat.)* Fine, you won; we'll start over tomorrow. *(She hangs up and crosses her arms.)* I'm all ears.

MURIEL. I was hoping it wouldn't have to be like this — me ... *dumping* on you as soon as I arrived. *(Pause. Muriel takes a deep breath.)* I would just talk to Daddy, but you know how he gets when he doesn't want to listen, and *will you stop looking at your watch?*

HAZEL. Will you start cutting to the chase?

MURIEL. *(Beat.)* I think Norm and I should take over the theater. *(Hazel just looks at her.)* You know, buy it from Daddy. *(Hazel scoffs and shakes her head.)* I know the place has seen better days, God knows it needs work. But with a little time and money, and ... *love*, we can fix everything that needs to be fixed.

HAZEL. Why?

MURIEL. Well, with Daddy's health, he's got to retire soon; this would give him a nest egg.

HAZEL. Why you?

MURIEL. Well, Norm doesn't really need to work anymore. He's been talking about selling some stock and —

HAZEL. Not Norm, not Dad, why *you*, Muriel?

MURIEL. Me?

HAZEL. Yeah, the one who drove here from Notre Dame to broach the deal.

MURIEL. *(Beat.)* You'll just think I'm crazy.

HAZEL. Of course you're crazy, it's a stupid idea.

MURIEL. That's not what I mean.

HAZEL. *Why you?*

MURIEL. *(Beat.)* I've been hearing things.

HAZEL. *(Beat.)* What are you talking about?

MURIEL. I've been *hearing* things. Voices. *(Beat.)* Forget it, you think I'm crazy ...

HAZEL. What do you mean voices?

MURIEL. I mean *voices*, people's *voices*. *(Hazel just looks at her.)* It started, I don't know, three weeks ago, in the middle of the night ...
HAZEL. You were dreaming.
MURIEL. *I was wide-awake*, but I started to hear them in the daytime too. Whispers ... when it's quiet, or ... nobody's home. *(Beat.)* I can't sleep, Hazel; I can't think. I keep the TV on all day, try to chase them out of my head.
HAZEL. And these voices tell you to buy real estate?
MURIEL. *They're little girls, Hazel. (Beat.)* Little girls' voices. *(Pause.)* For a while I figured, "Oh it's just me thinking about Laura and Katie as kids," you know, now they're both off at school. But yesterday, when I started back to Houston, I could finally make out what they were saying: *(Intently, to Hazel.)* It was all about flying, and faraway islands. *(As if to jar Hazel's memory.)* Singapore ... Cyprus ...
HAZEL. Have you seen somebody about this?
MURIEL. Today there was a woman's voice, too ...
HAZEL. *Have you seen somebody —*
MURIEL. They're us, Hazel;
HAZEL. No, we're us.
MURIEL. as little girls. And Mom.
HAZEL. *(Returning to work.)* I am not having this conversation ...
MURIEL. I knew I had to come home, get things back to the way they were. Something's happening, Hazel!
HAZEL. *(Facing off.)* Something certainly is: It's called change of life.
MURIEL. *(Beat.)* What's that supposed to mean?
HAZEL. Those hormones will do crazy things to your head.
MURIEL. This isn't about change of life ...
HAZEL. Honey, I know a hot flash when I see one.
MURIEL. This isn't about — have you been listening?
HAZEL. More than I'd like. *(Hazel returns to work.)*
MURIEL. I want you to talk to Daddy with me, about the theater.
HAZEL. No.
MURIEL. Why not?
HAZEL. Because I don't like you.
MURIEL. That's not true.
HAZEL. I haven't liked you since we were kids.
MURIEL. Well maybe it's time we tried to get along ...

22

HAZEL. Well maybe I don't feel like it anymore.

MURIEL. Well maybe you should.

HAZEL. Well maybe we ought to just call it a wrap. *(Mike appears, unnoticed, in the doorway.)* I've been hearing our voices, too, Muriel — they've been jabbering on for the last twenty minutes, and I'd really, really like them to stop. So how about you just drop this idea, drive back to Houston and find a good specialist who can help you out?

MURIEL. *(Beat.)* No.

MIKE. Mrs. Palmer?

MURIEL. I can't go back there. Not yet.

HAZEL. Why, Norm'll tell you you wasted some gas?

MURIEL. He ... doesn't know I'm here.

MIKE. *(Beat.)* Mrs. Palmer?

MURIEL. *(Still looking at Hazel.)* What.

MIKE. My dad wants popcorn too.

MURIEL. *(Beat.)* Can't he just share with your mom?

MIKE. They're divorced.

MURIEL. *(Beat.)* They're...? *(Beat.)* Oh. Sorry.

MIKE. No biggie.

MURIEL. I ... thought they —

MIKE. Yeah; no.

MURIEL. Sure, I'll ... Tell him I'll be right down. *(Mike exits. After a moment, Muriel makes her final push:)* Will you help me?

HAZEL. Why doesn't Norm know —

MURIEL. Just tell me, will —

HAZEL. I already told you —

MURIEL. I'm a little lost, Hazel. *(Beat.)* I need to find my way now, and I can't go back until I do. I'm just a little lost, that's all. *(Beat.)* Look, this has gone on thirty *years* ... Isn't it time we —

HAZEL. Thirty-one.

MURIEL. *(Beat.)* All right, thirty-one. *(Hazel turns away and occupies herself. Long pause.)* "Pilot to navigator. Come in navigator." *(Hazel stops working, but does not look up. Pause.)* "Pilot to navigator, come in navigator." *(Beat. Hazel turns to face Muriel. Pause.)* Now you say: "Navigator here ... " *(The two women simply look at each other as lights fade.)*

23

Reel Two

In darkness, the little girls' voices again, this time accompanied by the voice of a woman. As before, the voices have a hushed, reverent tone. In the blackout, the projector remains running.

WOMAN. *(V.O.)* Are you ready?

GIRL #1. *(V.O.)* Uh huh.   GIRL #2. *(V.O.)* Yes.

WOMAN. *(V.O.)* Okay. Where shall we go tonight? *(Beat.)*

GIRL #1. *(V.O.)* Singapore.

WOMAN. *(V.O.)* Muriel? *(Pause.)*

GIRL #2. *(V.O.)* I don't know.

WOMAN. *(V.O.)* Look at the map. *(Pause.)*

GIRL #2. *(V.O.)* Here.

WOMAN. *(V.O.)* Tierra del Fuego?

GIRL #2. *(V.O.)* Yes.

WOMAN. *(V.O.)* Okay — Tierra del Fuego and Singapore ...

GIRL #1. *(V.O.)* Singapore first.

WOMAN. *(V.O.)* All right — Singapore, then Tierra del Fuego ... *(Lights up on the projection room on a weekend night in the early 1950s. Except for the absence of a few props, such as the Trivial Pursuit game, it looks identical to the previous scene. After a moment, a young man enters swiftly and crosses toward the bathroom. His clothes, slick hair, and dark-rimmed glasses should place him squarely in the period.)*

NORM. Wait a second, I gotta flush. *(He disappears into the bathroom and shuts the door. The sound of porcelain rattling on porcelain — the back of a toilet being lifted and replaced. A flush; he returns.)* Okay, I'm done. *(Pause.)* You can come in now.

YOUNG MURIEL. *(Off.)* Maybe I shouldn't.

NORM. Why not — you think I got germs? *(He exits into the stairway.)*

YOUNG MURIEL. *(Off.)* I'm really not supposed to be up here, Norm.

NORM. *(Off.)* That's bullcrap. Hazel's up here all the time.

YOUNG MURIEL. *(Off.)* Well, she's Hazel.

NORM. *(Off.)* Like your old man'll notice while he's fixing a leak in the ladies' lounge.

YOUNG MURIEL. *(Off.)* Well ... all right. *(Young Muriel enters in a period skirt and blouse and carrying a bag of popcorn. She freezes in the center of the room, almost immediately struck by the memory of the place. With Norm behind her in the doorway, the image should mirror the opening of the play.)*

NORM. I wasn't supposed to be on tonight, but Joey Flynn broke his foot playin' ball, so. *(Beat.)* You okay? *(Beat.)* Hey Muriel.

YOUNG MURIEL. Huh?

NORM. You okay?

YOUNG MURIEL. Oh. Yeah.

NORM. You look like you just seen a ghost or somethin'.

YOUNG MURIEL. *(Embarrassed.)* Oh. No, I just ... haven't been up here in a long time.

NORM. Pretty different?

YOUNG MURIEL. *(Looking around again.)* Everything's different up here.

NORM. I can believe that. Look, you can even write your name in the dust.

YOUNG MURIEL. I brought you some popcorn.

NORM. How come?

YOUNG MURIEL. For letting me use your bathroom.

NORM. That's nothin'.

YOUNG MURIEL. Sure it is. *(She hands him the bag.)*

NORM. Thanks.

YOUNG MURIEL. *(Beat.)* I'll be done in a second.

NORM. Take your time. *(Young Muriel enters the bathroom and shuts the door. After a moment, Norm nonchalantly works his way over to the door and quickly glances through the keyhole, almost immediately snapping back to the projector. He stuffs a handful of popcorn into his mouth. Young Muriel reenters.)*

YOUNG MURIEL. I'll just wait till I get home.

NORM. *(Through popcorn.)* Huh? Why?

YOUNG MURIEL. There isn't any toilet paper.

NORM. Oh. Well, I'll go down and swipe a roll.

YOUNG MURIEL. Don't bother.

NORM. I mean it. I do it all the time.

YOUNG MURIEL. 'sokay. I don't have to go that bad.

NORM. It's no big deal.

YOUNG MURIEL. 'sokay. *(They stand awkwardly for a moment.)* Well, I guess I'll see you later. *(She turns to go.)*

NORM. Stick around.

YOUNG MURIEL. I really shouldn't —

NORM. Yeahyeahyeah, I know.

YOUNG MURIEL. Hazel's stuck at the counter by herself.

NORM. Come on, five minutes. What are you gonna do downstairs — wait around for some fat guy to get hungry?

YOUNG MURIEL. Well …

NORM. When I'm finished the popcorn, then you can go.

YOUNG MURIEL. *(Beat.)* Okay. *(Pause.)* How is it?

NORM. Good. You want some?

YOUNG MURIEL. No thanks. I don't eat popcorn. *(She begins to move around, looking about the room.)*

NORM. Don't eat popcorn? How come?

YOUNG MURIEL. I don't like the sound it makes.

NORM. *(Beat.)* You mean like "pop-pop"?

YOUNG MURIEL. *No*, when you eat it. It's … squeaky.

NORM. Squeaky.

YOUNG MURIEL. You know, on your teeth. *(Beat.)* You think I'm weird.

NORM. *(Grinning.)* A little, yeah.

YOUNG MURIEL. So maybe I am. *(She continues looking around, perhaps at one of the projectors.)* What don't you eat?

NORM. I eat everything.

YOUNG MURIEL. Brussels sprouts?

NORM. I don't mind brussels sprouts.

YOUNG MURIEL. Succotash?

NORM. I love succotash!

YOUNG MURIEL. Huh. I guess you do eat everything.

NORM. You don't like succotash?

YOUNG MURIEL. It's okay, I guess. I just don't like the sound.

NORM. *(Beat.)* You don't like the sound it makes when you eat it?

YOUNG MURIEL. No, when you say it. I don't like the sound

of the word. *(Norm just chuckles and shakes his head.)* Now you really think I'm weird.

NORM. I don't care. *(He watches her as she continues looking around, settling on the moving projector.)*

YOUNG MURIEL. Could you show me how to work this?

NORM. Nah, it'd take too long.

YOUNG MURIEL. Who's in a hurry?

NORM. I thought you had to get back down.

YOUNG MURIEL. "Like Daddy's going to notice from the ladies' lounge" ... *(Norm grins.)*

NORM. Sure, I could show you a few things ... *(He tosses a popcorn kernel in the air and catches it in his mouth, then strolls to the R projector.)* Ever seen one of these up close?

YOUNG MURIEL. Only when I was little, when my mom ran the projectors.

NORM. Your mom did?

YOUNG MURIEL. Yeah.

NORM. *(Looking around.)* Not much of a playroom for two little girls.

YOUNG MURIEL. Oh, no, it was wonderful! We could go anywhere we wanted. Everything was different up here.

NORM. What do you mean "go anywhere you wanted"?

YOUNG MURIEL. Oh ... nothing. *(Young Muriel looks out the viewport. Norm looks around to see what he's been missing.)* *Wings Over Water's* terrific, don't you think?

NORM. I don't know. I haven't really watched it.

YOUNG MURIEL. You're kidding me!

NORM. *(Shrugging.)* Just when I'm lookin' for cue marks.

YOUNG MURIEL. I've seen it twelve times already — wait, is it twelve or...? This'll be thirteen. I haven't even seen the beginning yet, I'm always at the counter.

NORM. What's it about, some lady pilot?

YOUNG MURIEL. "*Some* lady pilot"? *Amelia Earhart* — the greatest ever.

NORM. I thought she died tryin' to go around the world.

YOUNG MURIEL. Well, maybe —

NORM. Then she couldn't have been that great.

YOUNG MURIEL. But, no but see, nobody really knows, *really*.

She just disappeared. Most people think she got lost looking for this tiny island, in the middle of the ocean? Some even think the Japs got her. But in the movie, see, she falls in love with her navigator — that's Philip Archer — and they find another island and land there and live. You know, happily ever after. *(Young Muriel looks out again.)*

NORM. *(Casting his vote.)* I think she died. *(Young Muriel watches intently. Norm observes her for a moment, then:)* Here, why don't you use the glasses? *(Norm removes a pair of 3-D glasses and puts them on her, then turns up the volume on an U. wall speaker. We hear the sounds of* Wings Over Water *softly underneath the following. [See pages at end of script for text.] As Young Muriel watches the screen, Norm watches her, noting her reaction. After a while:)* You like Philip Archer?

YOUNG MURIEL. Oh sure, he's swell. *(Pause.)*

NORM. You think he's good-looking?

YOUNG MURIEL. I think he's dreamy, don't you?

NORM. I don't know. *(Beat.)* You think he's better-looking than me? *(Young Muriel just gives him a "dream on" look.)* Never mind, I don't want to know. *(They chuckle and turn back to the screen. Pause.)*

YOUNG MURIEL. What about Charlotte Ayres?

NORM. What about her?

YOUNG MURIEL. You think she's good-looking?

NORM. She can fill out a sweater. *(She looks at him, perhaps disapprovingly.)* That's what my brother says, "She can fill out a sweater." But I think she's stuck-up.

YOUNG MURIEL. Why do you think she's stuck-up?

NORM. I don't know, some girls you can just tell. They're the type, you ask them the time, they say buzz off. *(Young Muriel nods vaguely, then looks out again. They watch some more. After a while:)*

YOUNG MURIEL. You think I'm prettier than Charlotte Ayres? *(Pause. He grins.)*

NORM. You can fill out a sweater. *(Young Muriel is embarrassed. After a beat, she turns to go.)*

YOUNG MURIEL. I ought to go.

NORM. Heyheyheyhey, I didn't mean it like that.

YOUNG MURIEL. That's okay ...

NORM. I mean, I meant it, but I didn't mean it like that.

YOUNG MURIEL. I need to get back.

NORM. I'm not finished your popcorn yet.

YOUNG MURIEL. Hazel's waiting for me.

NORM. You're much prettier than Charlotte Ayres. *(Young Muriel stops in her tracks at the threshold. Pause.)*

YOUNG MURIEL. Now you're just saying that.

NORM. Much prettier. I mean she's fine, she's pretty, but like I said, she's stuck-up, so that takes something away. But you, you're not stuck-up at all, so ... so that adds something.

YOUNG MURIEL. *(Beat.)* You're not eating your popcorn.

NORM. I'm eatin' 'em one at a time. *(He tosses a kernel in the air and catches it in his mouth. Young Muriel scrutinizes him.)*

YOUNG MURIEL. This the way you talk with Hazel?

NORM. Nah, we don't really talk.

YOUNG MURIEL. Then what do you two do up here all the time?

NORM. *(Beat.)* Why don't you ask her, since you girls are so tight?

YOUNG MURIEL. Maybe I did.

NORM. What did she say?

YOUNG MURIEL. *(Beat.)* A lot of stuff Daddy wouldn't want to hear. *(Beat. Then they chuckle, embarrassed. Young Muriel turns away to look out the viewport again. Norm turns down the sound, then considers her carefully.)*

NORM. You want something to drink?

YOUNG MURIEL. What do you mean?

NORM. *(Beat.)* Never mind. *(Beat.)* I hear you're gonna follow her to Bryn Mawr next year.

YOUNG MURIEL. Yeah.

NORM. Be a "coed."

YOUNG MURIEL. Where do you want to go?

NORM. I'm not going to college.

YOUNG MURIEL. Why not?

NORM. Why should I? What's it cost, couple hundred dollars a year?

YOUNG MURIEL. I don't know; I guess.

NORM. To be stuck in a class while a bunch of boring teachers go on about the past?

YOUNG MURIEL. Well, there's more to it than that ...

NORM. *(Picking a slim paperback off the splicing table.)* This book cost me a nickel, and I can read it while I work. That's like me getting paid to learn.

YOUNG MURIEL. *(Reading the cover.)* *Your Smarts Can Make Millions.*

NORM. It's part of a series. I already read three of them. And when I finish this one, I'll pick up the next, then another and another, till I know everything I need to know.

YOUNG MURIEL. Huh.

NORM. See, the guys who are really gonna make it in the '50s aren't studying Shakespeare at Bryn Mawr. They're thinking, "What next?" "Now, what do people need?" "3-D movies?" "Technicolor television?" They're burning their maps and heading into unknown territory!

YOUNG MURIEL. Holy moley!

NORM. The book says it better than me.

YOUNG MURIEL. No, no ... that was swell. You sound just like my mom.

NORM. Your mom used to talk about 3-D?

YOUNG MURIEL. *No* ... she talked about ... I don't know, how anything's possible — anything, really — if we just put our head and our heart into it.

NORM. Well that's all I'm saying!

YOUNG MURIEL. I know!

NORM. It's possible, everything's possible.

YOUNG MURIEL. That's what she always said.

NORM. Huh.

YOUNG MURIEL. Yeah. *(Pause. They are both grinning. Young Muriel turns away at last, embarrassed by the intimacy.)* We used to play this ... game up here. That she taught us.

NORM. What kind of game?

YOUNG MURIEL. Never mind ...

NORM. No, tell me.

YOUNG MURIEL. It's stupid, really.

NORM. Tell me. *(Pause.)*

YOUNG MURIEL. Well ...

NORM. Go on.

YOUNG MURIEL. If you turn out the lights? And sit next to the projector, and hold your arms out front like this? You can pretend you're flying a plane.

NORM. What made your mom think of that?

YOUNG MURIEL. I don't know. I guess 'cause it's dark in here, and there's the sound of the projector, you know, like an engine. And when you look through the viewport, it's like there's a whole nother world out there. *(She looks out.)*

NORM. Huh.

YOUNG MURIEL. *(Smiling at the memory.)* She used to let us put on this old leather helmet — the kind you can get at the Army-Navy? And then she'd have us imagine all kinds of places we wanted to go, stuff we wanted to do, and see ...

NORM. Like where?

YOUNG MURIEL. Oh, I don't know ... Sumatra, or Cyprus, or ... Tierra del Fuego.

NORM. *(Chuckling.)* I never even heard of it.

YOUNG MURIEL. It's on the map somewhere. And sometimes we'd just fly, it didn't matter where, we'd just ... fly. But you always knew there was someplace safe to land down there, in the middle of it all. *(Pause.)*

NORM. Show me what you used to do.

YOUNG MURIEL. No ... *(She moves away from the viewport.)*

NORM. Come on.

YOUNG MURIEL. It's silly.

NORM. No it isn't; show me.

YOUNG MURIEL. We promised.

NORM. What do you mean? Promised who?

YOUNG MURIEL. Anyway, it's just a girl thing, that's all.

NORM. I don't care, what'd you do?

YOUNG MURIEL. I can't ...

NORM. I'll show you how to run the projector. *(Pause.)*

YOUNG MURIEL. Really?

NORM. Yeah.

YOUNG MURIEL. Tonight?

NORM. Tomorrow, next day, whenever. *(Pause.)*

YOUNG MURIEL. Promise?

NORM. I promise.

YOUNG MURIEL. *(Beat.)* It's not like it's even that interesting ...

NORM. That's okay.

YOUNG MURIEL. *(Beat.)* Well ... I'd sit here, and Hazel would sit there.

NORM. On the stool.

YOUNG MURIEL. Yeah. *(Norm moves the stool into position behind the chair and sits on it.)*

NORM. Okay. Then what?

YOUNG MURIEL. I really should go. *(She turns away.)*

NORM. No, no, this is cute. Then what?

YOUNG MURIEL. *(Beat.)* Then Hazel —

NORM. Wait, we forgot to turn out the light. *(He gets up and turns it out. Now, lit only by light shining out the sides of the projector, the room looks eerie and mysterious.)* There we go. Then Hazel what?

YOUNG MURIEL. Then Hazel would say —

NORM. Sit down. *(Norm takes her hand and gently pulls her onto the chair in front of him.)* What's she say?

YOUNG MURIEL. *(Reverently, as if invoking a great spirit.)* She says, "Pilot to navigator, come in navigator."

NORM. If she's the pilot, how come she's behind you?

YOUNG MURIEL. Well, these old planes, the pilot sat in the back.

NORM. Oh, yeah. *(Norm holds his arms out front as if gripping the stick of an airplane. As she goes through the ritual, he watches her with amused fascination.)*

YOUNG MURIEL. Then I say, "Navigator here," and she says, "Prepare for night flight." I don't think they say that in real life, but my mom taught us to say it like that, so we always do. Did. *(Beat.)* Then we'd just go on like that for a while and pretend we're flying.

NORM. Go on.

YOUNG MURIEL. You don't really want to hear this ...

NORM. Yeah I do.

YOUNG MURIEL. Not really.

NORM. Yeah. I do. *(Pause. Young Muriel takes a deep breath.)*

YOUNG MURIEL. Okay, but ... do me a favor? *(Norm lowers his arms.)* Don't tell Hazel we did this?

NORM. How come?

YOUNG MURIEL. *Just don't*, okay?

NORM. *(Backing off.)* Okay, okay ... *(He holds his hands out front again.)* So then what?

YOUNG MURIEL. Then she says, "All electric power off, radio

off," and I repeat it. Then —

NORM. "All electric power off, radio off."

YOUNG MURIEL. Right. *(Young Muriel mimes working the control panel of an aircraft.)* Then, "All controls adjusted and trimmed, check."

NORM. "All controls adjusted and trimmed, check."

YOUNG MURIEL. *(Miming.)* Ailerons normal position, check.

NORM. "Ailerons normal — "

YOUNG MURIEL. You can just say "check."

NORM. Okay, check.

YOUNG MURIEL. *(Miming.)* Elevators normal position, check.

NORM. Check. *(He rests his forearms on her shoulders. She turns her head toward him.)* My arms got tired. *(She faces front again.)*

YOUNG MURIEL. Prime engines.

NORM. Engines primed.

YOUNG MURIEL. *(Miming.)* Number one and number two mixture rich.

NORM. Check.

YOUNG MURIEL. Crank engine one.

NORM. *(Leaning forward.)* Check. *(She is very aware of his body behind her.)*

YOUNG MURIEL. Um ... crank engine two. *(She looks out the viewport.)*

NORM. Check.

YOUNG MURIEL. *(Suddenly.)* Oh, this part is the best! Can you turn it up?

NORM. Huh?

YOUNG MURIEL. The big love scene. Can you turn up the sound?

NORM. Uh ... sure. *(He crosses to the speaker and turns up the sound. As before, the tinny sounds of* Wings Over Water *are heard, along with a low airplane hum. He sits down again and leans forward as they both look out the viewport. As they watch the movie, Norm slowly slips his arms around Young Muriel's shoulder.)*

CARL. *(V.O.)* Why don't you try the radio again?

AMELIA. *(V.O.)* I've tried and tried, but there's no response.

CARL. *(V.O.)* Then try again, it's our only hope.

AMELIA. *(V.O.)* KHAQQ calling Itasca. We must be on you but cannot see you ... Gas is running low. Been unable to reach you

33

by radio. We are flying at altitude 1000 feet, over. *(Beat.)* When you took our bearings through the clouds, are you sure you caught the North Star?

CARL. *(V.O.)* My sextant doesn't lie. *(Suddenly, the airplane hum begins to sputter and the movie music turns dramatic. At the same time, Norm moves in for a kiss, slipping his hand over Young Muriel's breast. She bolts instantly, heading towards the stairway. The following happens very quickly.)*

NORM. Sorry, I'm sorry ...

YOUNG MURIEL. No ...

NORM. *(Grabbing her hand as she reaches the doorway.)* Don't go, please ...

YOUNG MURIEL. Let —

NORM. Come on ...

YOUNG MURIEL. Norm ...

NORM. You'll miss the best part.

YOUNG MURIEL. I've seen it twelve —

NORM. Not from up here.

YOUNG MURIEL. I really gotta —

NORM. It's different up here.

YOUNG MURIEL. Yeah, but —

NORM. Everything's different up here. *(Beat.)* Come on. *(She hesitates for a moment.)* I'm sorry, okay? *(By now the onscreen dialogue has continued. Young Muriel guardedly relents, sitting down again, slightly more alert than before. But the movie casts its spell.)*

AMELIA. *(V.O.)* We're down to the reserve tank. Twelve gallons, that's all.

CARL. *(V.O.)* That gives us less than twenty minutes. *(Pause.)* Aren't you frightened?

AMELIA. *(V.O.)* I'd been trying not to notice.

CARL. *(V.O.)* Well I'm frightened. Flying on fumes, a thousand feet above the largest, deepest ocean in the world ... You'd have to be a hero or a fool not to be frightened.

AMELIA. *(V.O.)* Which am I?

CARL. *(V.O. Beat.)* You're no fool, Amelia ... *(The romantic music begins once more. Norm again leans in close to Young Muriel.)* Last night, in the hangar, the way you looked ... those flowers that native boy placed in your hair ...

AMELIA. *(V.O.)* Please, Carl, not now.

CARL. *(V.O.)* You were waiting for me to kiss you, weren't you? *(Beat.)* Well, I wanted to kiss you; I should have kissed you, only …

AMELIA. *(V.O.)* Only what?

CARL. *(V.O.)* You know what; we both know.

AMELIA. *(V.O.)* Well, what's past is past. We can't live yesterday over again.

CARL. *(V.O.)* Maybe we can. *(Beat.)* According to the chronometer, in two minutes, we'll cross the 180th parallel.

AMELIA. *(V.O.)* The International Date Line …

CARL. That's right. On this side it's Monday, but over there it's Sunday — the day we left New Guinea, the day we should have kissed but didn't.

AMELIA. *(V.O.)* Oh, Carl … *(Norm turns Young Muriel's face towards him. They look at each other. Uncertain, she turns back to the screen.)*

CARL. *(V.O.)* Kiss me, Amelia. Kiss me all the way to yesterday.

AMELIA. *(V.O.)* What difference will it make? If the fuel runs out —

CARL. *(V.O.)* Then let it run out. I love you.

AMELIA. *(V.O.)* Oh, do you really mean it?

CARL. *(V.O.)* I've loved you to the stars, I'll love you to the bottom of the sea … *(Norm kisses Young Muriel as their onscreen counterparts also kiss, billowed by swelling romantic music. Young Muriel responds. Norm starts to put his hand over her breast again, but she deflects it deftly. Suddenly, a light, clear bell begins ringing, perhaps once per second. Young Muriel opens her eyes and looks around, amazed, though she keeps on kissing. Finally, she shuts her eyes again and eventually the bell stops. The movie soundtrack continues under the rest of the scene.)*

YOUNG MURIEL. Um … I think I really better go now.

NORM. We got three more reels left …

YOUNG MURIEL. I know, but —

NORM. Three more reels.

YOUNG MURIEL. Okay, but —

NORM. Hey listen:

YOUNG MURIEL. What about Hazel?

NORM. *Listen* … *(She looks at him.)* Just kiss me, all right? *(Beat.)* Just kiss me. *(She does. Lights fade.)*

Reel Three

Lights rise on the projection room, the night after Reel One. Muriel, wearing 3-D glasses, sits on the high stool by the R projector, looking out at the screen through the viewport. Her feet rest on the chair in front. Hazel works at the splicing table.

MURIEL. I never get to go to the movies anymore. Norm says, "It's a waste of time to sit in a dark room staring at a wall." Now he's building this huge cable network so people can stare at the idiot box ... *(Pause. Muriel checks her watch, then looks out again, smiling in remembrance.)* Couple years back, for my birthday? He said he wanted to take me to the movies. That might seem cheap for somebody else, but I was *so* excited. So we get dressed up — I mean really to the nines — and head off to see *King Kong*, that remake with Jessica Lange? But, in the car he says he has to drop off a file at Jerry Gilman's on the way to the theater. Jerry's his partner.

So fine, no problem, we've got almost fifteen minutes till the movie ... So we stop off at Jerry's and Norm runs in, and the motor's running, and any second he's coming back out, right? The man is nothing if not punctual. Five minutes go by, then ten. Then twenty ... I check my makeup in the rearview mirror and see this pitiful, overdressed woman waiting for a movie about a gorilla. And I realize I'm shaking, I'm so furious; I'm just ...

So I *fling* open the door and *march* to the house, and just *barrel* in ready to tell Norm and Jerry to, I don't know, *screw* themselves ... And there's, oh, twenty-five, maybe thirty people there, big grins, drinks in hand, couple of cameras. "Surprise!" As if I hadn't already wet myself. I was so *thrown* I didn't know whether to laugh or cry, so I just swallowed it and we had a party. Sort of.

Halfway through I noticed all these people were Norm's friends, from work. And their wives. I looked around that great big room and wondered, "Where are my friends, why didn't Norm invite ... " And then I realized *I* don't have any. *We* have friends, and that's who they are: Norm's friends. From work. And their wives. *(Pause.)* I guess in the end, though, he got the big surprise. *(Pause. Muriel watches the movie. Hazel looks up; in spite of herself, she can't not know the end to the story.)*

HAZEL. How?

MURIEL. By the time we left, around two A.M., the car had run out of gas and the battery was dead. We had to get towed all the way back to River Oaks. *(Pause.)* I never did see *King Kong*; was it any good?

HAZEL. It was better the first time.

MURIEL. Isn't it always ... *(Muriel looks at her watch, then out the viewport for a few moments, then back at Hazel.)* What went wrong with you and Ray?

HAZEL. *(Beat.)* Ray.

MURIEL. I mean, was it a gradual thing, or —

HAZEL. I don't want to talk about it. *(Hazel continues working.)*

MURIEL. It's just, you two always seemed *so good* together. I never saw anybody laugh so much. You shared so many things, little things ...

HAZEL. Muriel ...

MURIEL. I thought if anyone would go the distance —

HAZEL. Have you noticed you've been having a one-sided conversation?

MURIEL. *(Beat.)* I guess I'm used to it. *(Pause.)* I mean, you must still care about him ...

HAZEL. *Muriel* ...

MURIEL. You've got his picture on the wall!

HAZEL. There's a pushpin through the crotch. *(Beat. Muriel crosses to the wall and looks at it.)*

MURIEL. You're right, there is.

HAZEL. I call it "suburban voodoo." *(Muriel turns and watches Hazel work. Pause.)*

MURIEL. How long have you two been —

HAZEL. What did you promise when I let you come up here?

MURIEL. *(Beat.)* I'd sit on the stool and watch the movie.

HAZEL. And?

MURIEL. And leave you alone. *(Hazel points to the stool. Muriel dutifully sits and looks out. After a moment, she checks her watch again.)* I wonder if Norm's mad at me. For just taking off — do you think? (Beat.) I gave his secretary the number, said I'd be up here … *(Pause.)* I'll bet he's mad. *(Pause. Muriel regards Hazel carefully before speaking.)* I talked to Daddy last night, about the theater.

HAZEL. Did you.

MURIEL. He said he liked the idea. *(Hazel looks up skeptically.)* Well, not in so many words. But he seemed to like it. *(Hazel shakes her head and returns to work.)* Well he didn't say *no* … If we both talked to him, he'd have to consider it. *(She looks out the viewport.)* As it is, he just keeps the lights down low so people won't see the mildewed curtains, or the holes in the ceiling where the plaster's coming off. As if you could make what's falling apart go away by simply ignoring it. *(Beat.)* Remember how we used to brush the seats?

HAZEL. *(Beat.)* "Brush the seats"?

MURIEL. On Saturday nights.

HAZEL. I never brushed a seat in my life.

MURIEL. Yes you did, you just don't want to remember. *(Muriel looks out the viewport for a moment, then:)* Oh — I ran across something in Mom's room last night, you'll never guess. *(She crosses to her handbag.)* Look. *(Muriel holds up an old leather flying helmet; Hazel stares icily at her.)* I couldn't believe my eyes.

HAZEL. Where'd you find that?

MURIEL. *(Beat.)* In the top of the closet, with her —

HAZEL. Put it back.

MURIEL. *(Beat. Hurt, defensive:)* I will … *(Muriel sets the hat down on the high stool, then rests her hands on the stool, considering it. After a moment:)* I wish we could fly somewhere again. *(Hazel continues working.)* Like … Madagascar? Or Tierra del Fuego? *(Muriel looks back at Hazel.)* What do you say, Hazel? Couldn't we fly to Tierra del Fuego?

HAZEL. *(A warning.)* Muriel …

MURIEL. Just once?

HAZEL. You don't want to walk down Memory Lane.

MURIEL. Why not?

HAZEL. 'Cause if you're gonna walk down Memory Lane, you better be willing to make every stop. *(Hazel returns to work. Muriel looks out again.)*

MURIEL. I don't even know if it's nice in Tierra del Fuego. I just like the sound of the word ... *(Norm appears, as at the top of Reel Two, crossing from the door to the bathroom. Neither woman sees him.)*
NORM. Wait a second, I gotta flush.
MURIEL. What?
HAZEL. What. *(Muriel turns around just as Norm has disappeared into the bathroom.)*
MURIEL. Did you say something?
HAZEL. I thought you were talking for both of us. *(Muriel, a bit frightened, gives her head a quick, slight shake, as if to dispel this latest "voice." Then:)*
MURIEL. When Norm and I take over the theater —
HAZEL. Christ, not this again ...
MURIEL. Well, why shouldn't we? We've got the money ...
HAZEL. Look out this viewport. Tell me how many people you see.
MURIEL. I know attendance is down ...
HAZEL. Look out this viewport and tell me / how many people you see.
MURIEL. *I know attendance is down*, but that's because it needs work. If we fix it up, like the way it was —
HAZEL. You'll wind up with a beautiful, empty shrine to the Golden Age of Cinema.
MURIEL. People don't come because it looks rundown.
HAZEL. No, people don't come because we show old movies, so the only ones who'd want to come are old themselves, and half of *them* are *dead* so they couldn't come anyway.
MURIEL. They're not that old ...
HAZEL. *Look at them*, Muriel. They're all getting senior citizen discounts. We make more on popcorn.
MURIEL. Well do you have a better idea?
HAZEL. I do. *(She turns to go back to work.)*
MURIEL. *(Beat.)* What is it?
HAZEL. You won't like it.
MURIEL. Tell me. *(Beat. Hazel turns back to her.)*
HAZEL. Make it a multiplex.
MURIEL. *(Beat.)* That's disgusting!
HAZEL. Told you.
MURIEL. Hazel ...

HAZEL. Put *Porky's Two* on one screen, *Star Trek Three* on another, *Rocky … Twelve* on a third.

MURIEL. Please tell me you're joking.

HAZEL. It's survival. This place is a barn. You think we'll stay open showing cheesy old movies to a dozen geriatrics a night?

MURIEL. You're talking about classic motion pictures.

HAZEL. Tomorrow night is *Abbott and Costello Meet Frankenstein.*

MURIEL. And next week is *Casablanca.*

HAZEL. Which is two bucks across the street, and you can pause it when you need to use the bathroom. *(Beat.)* Welcome to the eighties. Men used to wear *suits* to the movies, and women wore dresses, when it cost a quarter instead of four-fifty. Now we're showing the same old flicks, but they dress like slobs and we fill twenty of a thousand seats. So what does that say about supply and demand?

MURIEL. Well, I'm talking to Daddy about my idea.

HAZEL. Go ahead and talk; I've talked to him too. *(Hazel works. Muriel looks at her.)*

MURIEL. You have?

HAZEL. Twice. He said he like the idea.

MURIEL. You're kidding.

HAZEL. "Well he didn't say no … " *(Beat.)* Give it up. You know in the end he'll do whatever he wants. Hell, he bought the place without asking his wife; what makes you think he'd consult his daughters? *(The telephone buzzes.)*

MURIEL. *(Relieved.)* There's Norm. *(Muriel walks toward the wall phone.)*

HAZEL. My phone my phone *my room my rules.* (Muriel stops before picking it up. Hazel goes to the wall phone and lifts the receiver.) Yeah, Mike. *(Beat. She looks at Muriel.)* Thanks. Tell him I'll be right with him. *(Hazel pushes a button, hangs up, returns to her splicing table, and resumes work.)*

MURIEL. Why did you hang up?

HAZEL. It's Ray.

MURIEL. Ray? Oh, it's — oh. *(Muriel respectfully returns to her stool, looks out, and waits for Hazel to pick up. When she doesn't, Muriel looks back at her and sees she is apparently absorbed in work.)* Hazel, what are you doing?

HAZEL. Running up his long-distance bill. *(Muriel gets it, then nods, understanding. Finally, Hazel finishes whatever she's doing and picks up the phone.)* You were supposed to call me last night. *(Beat.)* You liar, I was here at seven-thirty. *(Beat.)* Well of course I wouldn't be here at seven-thirty your time. *(To Muriel.)* The man's an idiot. *(Into phone.)* You're an idiot, Ray. *(Beat.)* You know why I want to talk to you, because I can't afford to drag you into court. *(To Muriel.)* Don't touch that. *(To phone.)* Not you — Muriel. *(Beat.)* Of course my sister, how many Muriels do you know? *(Beat. To Muriel:)* Ray says hi.
MURIEL. Hi Ray.
HAZEL. *(To phone.)* Muriel says hi. Look, we just have to settle who gets which appliance and sign a piece of paper. *(Beat.)* It's called "irreconcilable differences"; grown-ups who hate each other do it every day. *(Beat.)* When? *(Beat.)* Hold on, let me check my calendar. *(Hazel pushes a button on the phone and hangs up.)* He's flying in from Berkeley for a couple days next week. Wants to talk about it over dinner.
MURIEL. Oh. *(Pause.)* Maybe you can settle things then. *(Hazel nods, but does not move. Pause.)* Aren't you going to check your calendar?
HAZEL. I don't keep a calendar, you kidding? What am I going to write in a calendar?
MURIEL. Then why are you ... oh ...
MURIEL and HAZEL. ... phone bill.
MURIEL. Right. *(Hazel picks up the phone again and pushes a button.)*
HAZEL. What day do you have in mind? *(Beat.)* No, I can't do it then. *(Beat.)* Sorry, that's booked up, too. *(Beat.)* Nope, full. *(Beat.)* Full ... *(Beat.)* Tuesday? Mmm, that might be possible, if I move some things around. *(Beat.)* Fine, I'll meet you there. *(Beat.)* I just hope we can settle this like adults. Or in your case, adulterers. *(Muriel looks up.)* Thank you, I know. *(Pause.)* I know that too. *(Beat.)* I know, Ray. *(Beat.)* You too. *(Hazel hangs up.)* He's horny.
MURIEL. *(Delicately.)* So, he cheated on you ...
HAZEL. He keeps saying, "I love you, I love you," trying to get me to say it back. *(Hazel goes for a cigarette.)* Well, "I love you" doesn't mean shit without "I'm sorry."
MURIEL. How did it happen?

41

HAZEL. Our family always did have trouble with apologies. *(Hazel lights up.)*
MURIEL. Hazel? *(Hazel just points to Muriel's stool. Muriel sits. Pause. Hazel smokes, then exhales deeply, looking out.)*
HAZEL. That woman was such a disappointment. If a man's going to have a midlife crisis, you'd think he'd have the decency to find some pert little coed named "Mitzi." This one looked like me. *(Beat.)* Only consolation was that *she* dumped *him* two months after we separated.
MURIEL. And you never tried getting back together? *(Hazel shakes her head.)* Counseling...? *(Hazel just laughs bitterly. Pause.)*
HAZEL. Ever break a good piece of china? Not the everyday crap, but the *really* delicate stuff, like Mom's. *(Muriel nods.)* Even if you collect all the pieces and glue them together, it's never the same. It might look fine to somebody else; hell, it might look fine to you. But you know deep down it's something in pieces. *(She grinds out her cigarette.)*
MURIEL. But, if this other thing is over —
HAZEL. It's broken, Muriel. Leave it alone. *(Hazel begins working again. After a beat, Mike enters suddenly with Brenda, an attractive teenager with big hair. They wear 3-D glasses. Brenda carries several video boxes.)*
MIKE. Hey.
MURIEL. Oh. Hello.
BRENDA. Hi.
HAZEL. Hey, Brenda.
MIKE. That's Mrs. Palmer.
MURIEL. Hi.
HAZEL. Cool shades.
MIKE. There was a ton left over, so we took 'em. *(Reaching into his jacket packet, he drops a fistful of 3-D glasses on the table.)*
HAZEL. Of course you did. You've got chocolate on your face. *(Mike wipes his mouth with his sleeve.)*
BRENDA. Other side. *(Again.)*
HAZEL. *(To Muriel.)* Mike's my surrogate son, aren't you sweetie?
MIKE. Can we have a beer?
HAZEL. No.
BRENDA. Told you.

MIKE. Why not? You've given me beer before.

HAZEL. I've given you sips before. You're too young to appreciate a mature addiction like alcohol.

MURIEL. *(To Brenda.)* What's that you've got there?

BRENDA. Just a bunch of videos.

MURIEL. Can I see? *(Brenda hands Muriel the video boxes.)*

MIKE. They were jam-packed over there tonight. But Brenda put these on hold, so.

MURIEL. *(Reading.) Alien?*

BRENDA. I've seen it like five times.

HAZEL. *(To Brenda.)* Hey, I hear UMass offered you a scholarship.

BRENDA. Yeah.

MIKE. She doesn't have to take it though.

BRENDA. Well ...

MIKE. You don't. She can still go wherever she wants.

MURIEL. *(To Mike, for Hazel's benefit.)* I noticed your friends came back tonight. I guess they really like the old movies, huh?

MIKE. I guess. Can I use your bathroom?

HAZEL. Sure. Just jiggle the ...

MIKE. Yeah, I know. *(Mike exits into the bathroom and shuts the door.)*

MURIEL. Ever seen a 3-D movie before?

BRENDA. *Jaws Three.*

MURIEL. Oh. I didn't know that was —

BRENDA. Yeah; it's pretty stupid.

MURIEL. What do you think of this one?

BRENDA. What is it? *(She looks out the viewport.)*

MURIEL. *Wings Over Water.* Philip Archer and Charlotte Ayres.

HAZEL. "With Fred MacMurray as Commander Thompson ... "

BRENDA. Huh. You ever seen *Alien?*

MURIEL. I don't think so. What's it about?

BRENDA. This alien like attaches itself to your face? And lays its eggs in your stomach, and if you try to cut it off? it bleeds like this acid all over the place. And then, when the eggs hatch, the baby alien busts out of your body, and there's like guts and blood coming out.

MURIEL. Sounds charming.

BRENDA. Yeah, it's pretty gross. *(To Hazel.)* Well, I better go back down — my mom's picking us up. *(Brenda shouts at the bathroom door:) I'll meet you downstairs.*

MIKE. *(Off.)* Okay. *(Brenda exits.)*

MURIEL. Well. I find that very encouraging. *(Hazel looks at her.)*

HAZEL. You lost me.

MURIEL. The fact that Mike's friends came back tonight. That young people would want to see a classic movie.

HAZEL. Muriel.

MURIEL. You heard him.

HAZEL. They aren't coming to watch the movie.

MURIEL. I saw them here yester —

HAZEL. *Muriel ...*

MURIEL. *What?*

HAZEL. They aren't coming to watch the movie.

MURIEL. Then what are they — ? *(Beat.)* Get out of here.

HAZEL. It's cheap, it's dark, and the men's room has a vending machine.

MURIEL. That's just cynical.

HAZEL. Well, what do you think? There's a cult following of teenage Fred MacMurray fans?

MURIEL. No, but —

HAZEL. These kids don't even know who Amelia Earhart was, much less Charlotte Ayres.

MURIEL. Oh, come on now.

HAZEL. Want to bet?

MURIEL. She's a role model for a whole generation —

HAZEL. Of course *we* know. She's all we ever heard about.

MURIEL. My daughters studied her in seventh grade.

HAZEL. Well these kids don't.

MURIEL. They must.

HAZEL. Want to bet?

MURIEL. They have to know who —

HAZEL. Bottle of Stoli says you're wrong. *(Pause.)*

MURIEL. *Amelia Earhart?*

HAZEL. Holy moley, bottle of Stoli, what do you say? *(The toilet flushes.)*

MURIEL. I don't even drink.

HAZEL. You can give it to me if you win. *(Mike enters from the*

44

bathroom.)
MIKE. Win what?
HAZEL. Wash your hands.
MIKE. Huh?
HAZEL. Hands. Your. Wash. Please. *(Mike gives her a look of disbelief.)* "Employees must wash hands before returning to work."
MIKE. That's restaurants.
HAZEL. No, that's anywhere, because it's disgusting if you don't.
MURIEL. Mike, we have a trivia question for you.
MIKE. Soviet Union.
MURIEL. *(Beat.)* What?
MIKE. Is it Geography?
MURIEL. No ...
MIKE. Oh, good; 'cause I suck at Geography.
MURIEL. Can you tell me who Amelia Earhart was?
MIKE. Sure. We studied her in seventh grade.
MURIEL. *(To Hazel, smugly.)* Really?
MIKE. She's that Civil War nurse, right? *(Pause.)*
MURIEL. Right.
MIKE. Yeah, we learned about her.
HAZEL. Thank you. Now wash your hands.
MIKE. Didn't she like start the Red Cross?
HAZEL. *(She pushes Mike back toward the sink.)* Wash.
MURIEL. Something like that. *(Muriel sits by the viewport.)*
HAZEL. Wait a second, wait a second, come here.
MIKE. What. *(Hazel leans towards him, sniffing.)*
HAZEL. You little rat, you were drinking my vodka ...
MIKE. No I wasn't.
HAZEL. Hell you weren't, I can smell it on you.
MIKE. You can't smell vodka.
HAZEL. Hell I can't.
MIKE. You said you couldn't, that's why you drink it.
HAZEL. I can smell anything over eighty proof. Wash. *(He does.)* That's the last time you use my toilet. *(To Muriel.)* You owe me a bottle of Stoli.
MIKE. I only drank a little.
HAZEL. Not you; Mrs. Palmer. *(Mike finishes washing his hands. The changeover bell begins ringing.)* When I was your age, all we

45

ever drank was Coke.

MIKE. You lie.

HAZEL. *Occasionally* rum and Coke; at least there was Coke in it. Now get out of here. *(Mike exits. Hazel inspects the remaining film. Half to herself:)* "Teacher says, every time a bell rings, an angel gets its wings."

MURIEL. You think that's such a good idea?

HAZEL. What.

MURIEL. Keeping liquor in the bathroom. With a teenager around. *(The bell stops.)*

HAZEL. It was hidden inside the back of the toilet.

MURIEL. You think that's a good idea?

HAZEL. Yeah, the water keeps it cold. Old projectionist trick … *(Back to work.)*

MURIEL. I mean, sips of beer are one thing, shots are another.

HAZEL. *(Half to herself.)* Christ …

MURIEL. I'm only speaking as a mother …

HAZEL. Oh, don't start pulling that shit.

MURIEL. What?

HAZEL. That "only as a mother," like it's some kind of trump card.

MURIEL. Well …

HAZEL. I was a mother once, too, remember?

MURIEL. Oh, please …

HAZEL. Who fed you and dressed you and tried to teach you the facts of life?

MURIEL. Okay, but —

HAZEL. You think he'd have taken you shopping for Kotex and bras?

MURIEL. That's not the same as raising your own.

HAZEL. Well, you married a man who wanted babies, I didn't.

MURIEL. Well you got to go to Bryn Mawr.

HAZEL. Well you should've come too.

MURIEL. Well I married Norm instead.

HAZEL. Well that's not my problem. *(Hazel breaks away to the view-port and watches for the coming cue marks. Long pause.)* Can you imagine what kind of job I'd have if I hadn't had an Ivy League education? … three … two … one … "blip." *(She pushes a button on the side of*

46

the projector, triggering the changeover, as in scene one. Pause.)
MURIEL. Why did you say that?
HAZEL. What.
MURIEL. That me marrying Norm isn't your problem.
HAZEL. It's not.
MURIEL. Who said it was a problem?
HAZEL. Who's hearing voices?
MURIEL. They're not connected.
HAZEL. How do you know?
MURIEL. Because I know! Look, if you're going to be mean, I'll
wait for his call downstairs ... *(Muriel goes for her jacket and purse.)*
HAZEL. You said you don't talk ...
MURIEL. I didn't.
HAZEL. You did.
MURIEL. Well we don't! Not as much as we used to ...
HAZEL. *(Beat. Quietly:)* He finding it somewhere else?
MURIEL. No.
HAZEL. Sure?
MURIEL. *(Beat.)* No. *(Hazel simply exhales and shakes her head,
then removes the full take-up reel from the first projector and takes it
back to the splicing area.)* It could just be my imagination ...
HAZEL. Yeah, I know the feeling. You, me and Mom got all the
imagination. *(Beat. Suddenly Norm appears again, crossing from the
door to the bathroom.)*
NORM. Wait a second, I gotta flush.
MURIEL. *(Turning.)* What? *(Hazel looks up at Muriel, who has
turned just in time to see Norm's back before it disappears into the
bathroom. She removes her glasses, confused and a little frightened, then
gives her head a quick, slight shake, as before.)* Did Mike come back?
HAZEL. Mike? *(Muriel approaches the doorway and pokes her head
inside.)*
MURIEL. That's odd. *(She looks at Hazel.)*
HAZEL. Oh, for God's sake ...
MURIEL. No, I *heard* somebody ... *(Muriel looks around warily.)*
HAZEL. You're starting to sound like Joan of Arc. *(Muriel is
stung.)* First little girls, then Mom ...
MURIEL. I *heard* them.
HAZEL. No. You got nostalgic for a silly old game and decided

47

to buy a silly old theater.

MURIEL. We can save the theater.

HAZEL. It's dead, Muriel, face it. Mommy's dead, the game is dead, the theater's dead.

MURIEL. We'll see about that.

HAZEL. By the sound of things, your marriage is dead.

MURIEL. I am working on my marriage.

HAZEL. Oh give me a break, why do women say that? It's like you've got it on blocks in the driveway ...

MURIEL. When we get this venture going —

HAZEL. It's dead, Muriel. And considering how you two got together, I'm not surprised. *(Hazel returns to work.)*

MURIEL. *(Beat.)* What do you mean by that?

HAZEL. Just what I said.

MURIEL. *(Beat.)* You mean Gloria Blakely's party? *(Beat. Hazel looks at her, then returns to work.)*

HAZEL. That's right, "Gloria Blakely's party."

MURIEL. You're still angry about me and Norm —

HAZEL. Is that what you think?

MURIEL. ... that he broke up with you and went with me.

HAZEL. Well, it's not like you ever apologized for it.

MURIEL. Yes I did.

HAZEL. Never. I keep track of these things.

MURIEL. After all this time, you still can't let / go —

HAZEL. You are such a goddamn liar, you / know that?

MURIEL. What are you — how dare you / call —

HAZEL. Talk about "Gloria Blakely's party" ...

MURIEL. We danced at Gloria Blake —

HAZEL. I've heard the story a hundred times, but that's not how you got together.

MURIEL. Yes it is.

HAZEL. You lie, Muriel.

MURIEL. We danced to "Kiss of Fire" by —

HAZEL. I saw you.

MURIEL. You weren't even there.

HAZEL. No, not at the party.

MURIEL. Then how can you say —

HAZEL. *I saw you.* Through the viewport. *(Muriel is speechless.)*

48

"Pilot to navigator, come in navigator." "Navigator here." *(Beat.)* Big kiss, fade out, happy ever after.

MURIEL. Oh God ...

HAZEL. Yeah. Easy to forget these work both ways. *(Pause. Hazel begins digging around for a cigarette.)*

MURIEL. Hazel, I ... I'm sorry.

HAZEL. There's that apology — better late than never.

MURIEL. We wanted to keep it secret until he broke up with you.

HAZEL. Don't even start ...

MURIEL. So it wouldn't seem like he left you just to be with me.

HAZEL. Will you shut up? I don't care that you kissed him, I don't even care that you married him.

MURIEL. So for thirty-one years you've —

HAZEL. *I saw you, Muriel.* Sit here and play our game with him — *our* game. Like it was "Spin the Bottle."

MURIEL. You said it was silly ...

HAZEL. It *wasn't* silly, not when it was the two of us. The three of us. Then it was something even Daddy couldn't touch.

MURIEL. But we hadn't played it in years.

HAZEL. Of course not, how could we?

MURIEL. Then why are —

HAZEL. *(Clutching the flying helmet in her fist.)* It's all we had left of her! *(Beat.)* It's all we had left and you pissed it away on a B-movie romance ... Let that arrogant shit be the pilot, too. *(She tosses the helmet back down. Beat.)* She wanted us to go so much farther than she did. And I promised we would. Guess we both failed. *(She starts toward the bathroom.)*

MURIEL. Hazel ... I'm sorry.

HAZEL. Save your apology. I'm not the one you betrayed. *(The phone buzzes.)* Well now, perfect timing; you can have the phone booth to yourself. *(She crosses to the bathroom.)*

MURIEL. Hazel ...

HAZEL. I'm having a drink. *(Hazel enters the bathroom. Muriel hesitates. The phone buzzes again. Off:)* Mrs. Palmer, your husband's waiting ... *(Muriel hesitates, then goes to the phone; but Hazel quickly reappears from the bathroom. Quiet, intense:)* Listen: You go ahead. Tell him about your great idea to save a theater and a marriage at the same time. I'll cut this place into thirds before you make it a

museum for your first kiss. *(Hazel returns to the bathroom. Muriel gathers herself, then picks up the phone.)*
MURIEL. Hello? *(Beat.)* Thanks, Mike. *(She pushes a button on the phone. Instantly, Norm enters through a wall, eating popcorn.)*
NORM. Pilot to navigator, come in navigator ...
MURIEL. *(Seeing him. Beat.)* Norm?
NORM. Navigator here.
MURIEL. *(Suddenly, to phone.)* Oh — Aunt Esther ...
NORM. All electric power off, radio off ...
MURIEL. *(To phone.)* Yes?
NORM. All controls adjusted and trimmed ...
MURIEL. *(To phone.)* Oh.
NORM. Ailerons normal position ...
MURIEL. *(To phone.)* Oh no ...
NORM. Elevators normal position ...
MURIEL. *(To phone.)* Oh God ...
NORM. Prime engines ...
MURIEL. But — *(Hazel reenters from the bathroom and listens.)*
NORM. Number one and number two mixture rich ...
MURIEL. Okay.
NORM. Crank engine one ...
MURIEL. Yes.
NORM. Crank engine two ...
MURIEL. All right.
NORM. Advance down runway! *(Muriel hangs up, shaken.)*
HAZEL. What did he say?
MURIEL. Um, no, that was Aunt Esther.
HAZEL. Esther?
MURIEL. Yeah, um ...
NORM. "Fasten your seat belt:"
MURIEL. Daddy had a stroke. *(Hazel looks at Muriel.)* He's dead.
NORM. "It's gonna be a bumpy night!" *(Hazel and Muriel just look at each other. Norm tosses a kernel of popcorn high in the air. Blackout.)*

End Act One

ACT TWO

Reel Four

The booth, a few days later. The R projector is rolling, the L is loaded with film. A colorful dress hangs on a hanger on the bathroom door. Mike, in his usher's uniform, argues on the phone while Hazel, wearing black, readies herself to go out, occasionally drinking from a glass on the table.

MIKE. *(On phone.)* You said you wouldn't. *(Beat.)* Couple weeks ago. You said you wouldn't decide till May. *(Beat.)* Okay, March. *(To Hazel.)* Roll me. *(Hazel rolls the die. Mike on phone.)* Well, when does UMass need to know? *(Beat.)* Then tell 'em then. If they don't need — *(Beat.)* I know, but you might change your mind.
HAZEL. Geography.
MIKE. *(Of roll.)* Shit.
HAZEL. Don't swear. *(Hazel pulls out a question card.)*
MIKE. *(On phone.)* Yeah, but a lot can happen between now and May. I *meant* March, look, all I'm saying — huh? *(Beat.)* Okay, okay ... *(Beat.)* No, go ahead. *(Beat.)* No, just ... fine. *(Mike holds the mouthpiece away from his mouth.)* She's got a bunch of customers. Can I roll again?
HAZEL. No.
MIKE. Come on, I'll let you roll again.
HAZEL. I don't have time to roll again, and neither do you. *(Hazel exits into the bathroom. Long pause. Mike holds the phone with one hand while he drums nervously with the other.)*
MIKE. There were a lot of people at the church, huh? *(Beat.)* You know everybody?
HAZEL. *(Off.)* Not everybody, no.
MIKE. Me neither. *(Pause.)* Mr. Brubaker looked good. I mean,

51

not good, but you know, considering. *(Beat.)* I'da worn black, too, if I had it, but all I got is this old blue leisure suit my dad used to wear, so. *(Hazel returns from the bathroom. Of his usher's uniform:)* This didn't look too stupid, did it? *(Hazel looks at him.)* I mean, since I had to go to work right after …

HAZEL. It's fine as long as you wear the tie.

MIKE. That's what I say. Brenda thought it looked stupid, but the leisure suit's even worse. *(Pause.)* And I woulda run the projector if you wanted.

HAZEL. I know.

MIKE. Not even threaded it up or nothin', just turned it on. So you could go to the cemetery.

HAZEL. That's okay. *(Hazel returns to the bathroom.)*

MIKE. *(Beat.)* 'Cause it seemed like they wanted you there and all. *(Beat. To phone:)* Huh? *(Beat.)* No, that's okay, so … *(Beat.)* Well how much are they giving you? *(Beat.)* Total. *(Beat.)* Okay, but see, La Salle's that much cheaper, and you can live at home. *(Beat.)* Well I don't either, but I am … *(Beat.)* Aw, come on … *(Beat.)* All right, forget it. No, just forget it. I'll see you. *(Mike hangs up and sits at the table. Hazel reenters.)* Let me roll again.

HAZEL. You ready?

MIKE. Come on, I'm so close.

HAZEL. *(Reading the question card.)* "What country contains the world's largest — ?"

MIKE. I suck at Geography.

HAZEL. Tough. "What country — "

MIKE. Let me do Entertainment.

HAZEL. *(Setting down the question card.)* Listen — as a would-be mother to her surrogate son I'm offering you this little bit of wisdom …

MIKE. *(Another lecture.)* Shut up …

HAZEL. And because you're so grateful for every tidbit, I'll give it to you for free:

MIKE. *(Reaching for the card.)* What's the question?

HAZEL. *(Holding the card away from him.)* You rolls your dice, you moves your piece, you takes your chances.

MIKE. *(Thoroughly bored.)* Soviet Union. *(Hazel looks at him for a second, then at the back of the card. She is shocked.)*

HAZEL. Son of a bitch ...

MIKE. *(Beat.)* That's right? *(He takes the card from her.)*

HAZEL. How'd you get that?

MIKE. *(Reading it.)* No shit.

HAZEL. Don't swear; did you look at the back?

MIKE. I always say Soviet Union. Give me a thingee.

HAZEL. Get your own thingee, I need to get dressed. Christ, look at the time ... *(Hazel takes the hanging dress into the bathroom. Mike retrieves a colored wedge from the game box and places it inside his piece.)*

MIKE. We're almost done.

HAZEL. *(Off.)* You better get yourself home.

MIKE. Just one round? *(Beat.)* Come on. *(Beat.)* I'll let you go next.

HAZEL. *(Off.)* Okay ... Roll me. *(Mike rolls, looks. Rolls again, looks. Muriel enters, wearing black.)*

MURIEL. Hi, Mike. *(He turns to see her.)*

MIKE. Oh, hi. *(Mike rolls again.)*

HAZEL. *(Off.)* What?

MIKE. *(To Hazel.)* Nothing. You got Geography, too.

HAZEL. *(Off.)* Soviet Union.

MIKE. *(Reaching for a card.)* I didn't read the question yet.

HAZEL. *(Off.)* Soviet Union.

MIKE. *(Reading the back of the card.)* No, Paraguay.

HAZEL. *(Off.)* So much for your strategy. *(Hazel reenters and sees Muriel.)* Oh, you're back.

MURIEL. Yeah.

HAZEL. How'd it go?

MURIEL. Not bad, for a burial.

HAZEL. *(To Mike.)* What was the question?

MURIEL. Though Aunt Esther *did* wonder why you had to run off like that.

HAZEL. *(Beat. To Mike:)* The question?

MIKE. "Bolivia is one of only two landlocked South American countries. Name the other."

HAZEL. Hmm — guess that couldn't be Soviet Union.

MURIEL. Did you hear what I said?

HAZEL. Yeah, Aunt Esther thinks I'm a rotten daughter.

MURIEL. I didn't say that.

HAZEL. No, but she did, didn't she? *(Mike rolls. Hazel drinks. Muriel is silent.)* Didn't she.

MURIEL. Have you been drinking?

HAZEL. Figured. *(Hazel picks a card.)* We had a matinee.

MIKE. *(None too pleased.)* Green.

HAZEL. "What's the difference between a Bactrian camel and a Sopwith Camel?" *(Pause. Mike thinks for a moment; then, completely stumped, chooses to abort.)*

MIKE. *(Standing suddenly.)* I better go.

HAZEL. Not even a guess?

MIKE. My mom's got dinner on the stove. See you later.

MURIEL. Bye. *(Mike exits; Hazel looks after him.)*

HAZEL. You know, I love him; but I'll tell you, that kid cheats worse than my husband.

MURIEL. It's nice to see you're taking this so well.

HAZEL. How do you mean?

MURIEL. I walk in and you're playing twenty questions.

HAZEL. Life goes on, Muriel.

MURIEL. *(Of her outfit.)* I can see that.

HAZEL. *(Off.)* Yeah, well, it's bad luck to wear black all day long. *(Hazel exits into the bathroom. Pause.)*

MURIEL. I came back to see if you'd change your mind about tonight. *(Beat.)* Everyone's going to be back at the house: my girls, the cousins, Aunt Esther, Norm …

HAZEL. *(Off.)* Some of us have to work tonight.

MURIEL. No you don't. *(Beat.)* I talked with Daddy's old projectionist, the one who retired?

HAZEL. *(Off.)* Yeah, I saw him.

MURIEL. He said he'd be glad to come in tonight. *(Pause. Hazel reenters but continues preparing to go out.)* Or we could just close …

HAZEL. We're not closing.

MURIEL. It's a Tuesday night, Hazel …

HAZEL. I'm the oldest, and I say we're not closing …

MURIEL. Then —

HAZEL. … besides, the Old Man would have wanted it this way. *(Case closed. They both know she's right. Hazel busies herself as Muriel exhales deeply and tries to restore civility.)*

MURIEL. I thought the service was nice, overall, don't you? Not too tacky. *(Beat.)* And Daddy looked good, that's the most important thing. At least he's with Mom now.

HAZEL. God, I hope not. *(Muriel looks at her.)* They never were very good together, or didn't you notice? *(Hazel returns to the bathroom. Off:)* Norm looked good, too.

MURIEL. Yes, he did.

HAZEL. *(Off.)* But why do bald men try to cover their entire head with their last three hairs? *(Pause.)*

MURIEL. I was hoping you and he and I would have a chance to talk.

HAZEL. *(Off.)* About what?

MURIEL. About the theater. *(Beat.)* I'm hoping you'll consider our offer.

HAZEL. *(Off.)* What offer?

MURIEL. If he wants to make an offer.

HAZEL. *(Off.)* You haven't even talked to him about it yet?

MURIEL. Well, I wanted to discuss it with you again first. Find out if you're still set on this … *multiplex* thing … *(Pause.)* Hazel, come back to the house. Please. It's silly for us to be open tonight. People will be expecting you there.

HAZEL. *(Reentering.)* They'll be expecting Ingrid Bergman here.

MURIEL. No, it's *wrong* for us to be open tonight. We should have been closed this afternoon.

HAZEL. I'll have you know, we've got thirteen people for *The Prisoner of Zenda.*

MURIEL. I don't care …

HAZEL. We're talking the remake.

MURIEL. I think it's shameful.

HAZEL. Well sure, the original's better, but —

MURIEL. Why are you doing this?

HAZEL. What.

MURIEL. *Boycotting* his burial, and the gathering tonight? All right, he wasn't a perfect father, *or* husband, but at least have some respect for the dead.

HAZEL. Like he did?

MURIEL. Oh, come on …

HAZEL. Keeping us away from her funeral?

MURIEL. That was / Aunt Esther's …
HAZEL. *(Simultaneous with Muriel.)* … Aunt Esther's idea, isn't it always? *(Beat.)* God forbid his daughters should see their mother again. And under such dreary circumstances. Better to say "she went to a better place" — that way they'll think she dropped off the edge of the earth … *(Hazel returns to the bathroom. Pause.)*
MURIEL. Why are you getting so dolled up?
HAZEL. *(Beat.)* Dinner engagement.
MURIEL. *(Beat.)* You've got a *date?*
HAZEL. Not in so many words.
MURIEL. I can't believe this …
HAZEL. Don't get excited. *(Hazel reenters with a vodka bottle.)*
MURIEL. Well, the timing seems a little bizarre, don't you think?
HAZEL. It's Ray.
MURIEL. Ray? I didn't see — holy moley, that's tonight?
HAZEL. That's right.
MURIEL. The divorce thing?
HAZEL. The separation agreement thing.
MURIEL. Good God, Hazel, couldn't you have canceled?
HAZEL. I didn't want to cancel, I want to get it over with.
MURIEL. I mean, with the funeral …
HAZEL. Can you stick around for fifteen minutes?
MURIEL. What?
HAZEL. There's a changeover coming; I'm already late.
MURIEL. Well, all right, but —
HAZEL. Just wait for the second blip and hit the button.
MURIEL. Maybe you should bring your lawyer or something.
HAZEL. I pay her too much as it is; if she starts getting dinners, she'll think I'm a patsy.
MURIEL. Still …
HAZEL. *(Toasting.)* To life, liberty, and the pursuit of happiness …
MURIEL. You never know what he'll say or do.
HAZEL. I've lived with the man half my life; I know what he'll order for dinner. *(Hazel fixes her hair in the mirror, vodka glass in hand.)*
MURIEL. Then at least keep your head clear. You shouldn't be drinking.
HAZEL. I know …

MURIEL. You shouldn't.

HAZEL. I know I shouldn't.

MURIEL. Then why are —

HAZEL. *Because I'm terrified.* Jesus. I haven't seen him since I moved out.

MURIEL. I know, that's why —

HAZEL. You don't know, Muriel, how could you know? You've never taken a stand in your life.

MURIEL. Yes I have ...

HAZEL. Oh the hell you have. You've always sat by and been the good daughter, or wife, or mother. Well I hate to tell you, but your kids are gone, your parents are dead, and you're waiting for your husband to take you to the movies!

MURIEL. I'm not waiting —

HAZEL. For God's sake, Muriel, you know how to drive, you can pay for a ticket. Just go to the movies!

MURIEL. By myself?

HAZEL. *(Beat.)* No, you're right: If you want to be a doormat, be a doormat ...

MURIEL. I am not a *doormat* ...

HAZEL. ... at least you're in front of a beautiful house. *(Hazel returns to the mirror and attempts to fix her hair.)*

MURIEL. Oh, and you're Ms. Gloria Steinem, huh? *(Hazel begins humming loudly to herself, ignoring her.)* With your "feminine independence" and your college degree. Well guess what, Bryn Mawr *isn't* Ivy League, it's Seven Sisters, even I knew that! *(Pause. Hazel continues humming.)* Are you listening to me? *(Hazel thrusts her hand into her purse.)*

HAZEL. Look at this, you see this? *(She pulls out a folded document of several pages and slams it on the table.)* This is a separation agreement. Designed to amputate my husband from the rest of my life.

MURIEL. So I guess that's a real achievement, huh? To kill off a man who'd cut out his heart for you, all because of a two-month affair.

HAZEL. Forget it ...

MURIEL. You think you're this powerful, liberated woman who's shaking off the shackles of marriage —

HAZEL. At least I'm doing / some —

MURIEL. ... but you're really just a bitter, disappointed housewife with a drinking problem.

HAZEL. Get out of here.

MURIEL. And while your only father's being put into the ground —

HAZEL. *Get out of my room.*

MURIEL. Why, what'll you do?

HAZEL. *Get out!*

MURIEL. Call up your union pals and tell 'em to kneecap me? *(Hazel goes back into the bathroom and slams the door.)* Oh, that's good, now slam the door. Just like when we were five. *(Muriel goes to the door.)* You act so tough, you talk like a lumberjack, but when you get down to it, you're no better than me. *(Pause.)* Listen, I know things aren't perfect with Norm, he's driven and ... selfish sometimes, and I've had to put some things on hold, but at least we've stuck it out. There's times I could have called it quits too. But I stuck it out. *(Pause.)* Look, I'm sorry I yelled at you; I'm just a little shook up today. Okay? *(Beat.)* Come on, open the door. *(Pause. She tries the door; it's locked.)* Hazel, open the door. *(Pause.)* Hazel? *(Beat.)* What are you doing?

HAZEL. *(Off.)* Fixing my fucking mascara.

MURIEL. There's a bigger mirror out here.

HAZEL. I don't want a bigger mirror. I see too much of my face as it is.

MURIEL. Well ... can you fix your mascara with the door open?

HAZEL. *(Off.)* I don't think so, no. *(Long pause.)*

MURIEL. I took a call for him a few weeks back. An associate of his from Reno who talks too loud and insisted on calling me Marion, or Marilyn, I forget. *(With Western twang.)* "Well ya see, Marion ... " "It's like this, Marion ... " I was just about to correct him when he brought up this "crazy weekend" he and Norm and I spent at the Denver Radisson last July. *(Beat.)* That's when I realized he probably meant Marion, or Marilyn, one or the other. I've never been to Denver in my life ... *(Pause.)* Are you listening, Hazel?

HAZEL. *(Off.)* Yeah, I heard you ... *(Norm appears, as before, crossing through the room.)*

NORM. Wait a second, I gotta flush.

MURIEL. *(Turning.)* What? *(She sees Norm just as he passes by her,*

opens the bathroom door, and disappears inside. The door shuts behind him. Muriel is terrified.)
HAZEL. *(Off. Louder.)* I said I heard you. *(The sound of porcelain rattling on porcelain.)*
MURIEL. Hazel ... Hazel, are you okay? *(Muriel tries the doorknob; it's still locked. The toilet flushes.)*
HAZEL. *(Off.)* I heard you, all right? Can you just let me try and resurrect my hair? *(Perplexed and frightened, Muriel turns to scan the room cautiously.)* I have got to get myself a new barber ... That man uses scissors like a martial art. *(Norm reenters from the bathroom. The door shuts behind him.)*
NORM. Okay, I'm done.
MURIEL. Oh Jesus ...
NORM. You can come in now.
MURIEL. Hazel?
HAZEL. *(Off.)* What?
NORM. Why not — you think I got germs? *(He exits.)*
MURIEL. *Hazel?*
HAZEL. *(Off.)* What?
MURIEL. Hazel!!
HAZEL. *(Opening door.)* What, what the hell...? *(Muriel looks after Norm, but he is gone. She gives her head a quick shake.)* What? *(Muriel looks back at Hazel.)*
MURIEL. You're not going to believe this ...
HAZEL. Oh, Christ, not again. *(Hazel moves back into the room.)*
MURIEL. No, this was different, this was ... 3-D. *(Hazel looks at Muriel.)* I've been seeing something, Hazel.
HAZEL. No you haven't.
MURIEL. Some*one.*
HAZEL. You buried your father this afternoon, so your head's a little warped ...
MURIEL. It's not about Daddy.
HAZEL. Yes it is.
MURIEL. No it's not ...
HAZEL. People die, then they're dead.
MURIEL. This isn't a dead person.
HAZEL. *(Back to her preparations.)* I'm not having this conversation ...

MURIEL. It's Norm. *(Hazel stops.)* Like he was when we met him. *(Hazel looks at Muriel for a moment, then walks briskly to her and slaps her.)*

HAZEL. Snap out of it, Muriel.

MURIEL. Why did you hit me?

HAZEL. 'Cause you're talking like a crazy lady.

MURIEL. I'm telling you, I saw —

HAZEL. And I'm telling you you're a little out of whack; and if you think I won't hit you again, you're wrong.

MURIEL. It's not the first time I — *(Hazel raises her hand and takes a step toward Muriel, who backs off quickly.)* It happened three days ago, when Aunt Esther called —

HAZEL. *(Giving up.)* I really don't have time for this. *(Hazel continues preparing herself.)*

MURIEL. *(Indicating the spot.)* He was right here.

HAZEL. I'm not listening …

MURIEL. Look I'm shaking I'm so —

HAZEL. Where's my blush? There it is.

MURIEL. You don't believe me.

HAZEL. *(To herself.)* Little bit of blush, bit of blush, bit of blush …

MURIEL. I swear to you, not even a minute ago —

HAZEL. Muriel. My dear hysterical sister. I believe I've got enough real world to hold my attention for the next two hours. I can't deal with the spirit world too. *(She gathers her things.)* "I'm ready for my close-up, Mr. DeMille … "

MURIEL. Don't leave me alone here.

HAZEL. Just hit the changeover button; otherwise, keep your hands off the projector.

MURIEL. Hazel …

HAZEL. Did you hear me? Projector. You. Touch. Don't.

MURIEL. *(Beat.)* What am I supposed to tell Aunt Esther?

HAZEL. Tell her I wanted to come, but I picked up a sailor. *(Hazel checks herself in the mirror one last time, then, noticing the photo of Ray, removes it, looks at it, and slips it into her pocket or purse. She turns to Muriel.)* Well. Wish me luck.

MURIEL. *(Quietly.)* Good luck. *(Hazel gives a quick, short nod in response and exits. Muriel looks after her for a while, then turns back into the room. She is wary, letting her eyes wander around, then occa-*

60

sionally snapping her head to the side as if she might glimpse some apparition in the corner. Eventually she settles down a bit. Almost immediately Norm appears again from the stairway.)

NORM. You okay? *(Muriel screams, wheeling around to see Norm and clattering into empty reels or film cans.)* Hey.

MURIEL. Oh God ...

NORM. You okay?

MURIEL. Why are you here?

NORM. You look like you seen a ghost or something.

MURIEL. *What do you want?*

NORM. Pretty different?

MURIEL. *(Beat.)* What?

NORM. Huh.

MURIEL. *(Half to herself.)* I've gotta get out of here ... *(Muriel makes a beeline towards the door.)*

NORM. Take your time. *(Muriel looks back, noticing that Norm is not even looking at her. Young Muriel enters from the bathroom, with popcorn. On seeing her, Muriel gasps.)*

YOUNG MURIEL. I'll just wait till I get home.

NORM. Stick around.

YOUNG MURIEL. I really shouldn't —

NORM. Yeahyeahyeah, I know.   MURIEL. Holy moley ...

YOUNG MURIEL. Hazel's stuck at the counter by herself.

NORM. Come on, five minutes. What are you gonna do down-stairs — wait around for some fat guy to get hungry?

YOUNG MURIEL. Well ... okay. I brought you some popcorn.

NORM. How come?

YOUNG MURIEL. For letting me use your bathroom.

NORM. That's nothin'.

YOUNG MURIEL. Sure it is. *(She hands him the bag.)*

NORM. Thanks. *(Young Muriel looks out the viewport.)*

MURIEL. Holy holy moley ... *(Muriel can't take her eyes off them. Throughout the following, Lights shift gradually over the course of minutes, making the room darker overall, with stark shadows, perhaps strange colors, all almost imperceptibly.)*

YOUNG MURIEL. *Wings Over Water's* terrific, don't you think?

NORM. I don't know. I haven't really watched it.

YOUNG MURIEL. You're kidding me!

NORM. *(Shrugging.)* Just when I'm lookin' for cue marks.

YOUNG MURIEL. I've seen it twelve times already — wait, is it twelve or…?

MURIEL. *(Half to herself.)* Thirteen.

YOUNG MURIEL. This'll be thirteen. I haven't even seen the beginning yet, I'm always at the counter. *(Young Muriel watches intently. Norm and Muriel observe her for a moment.)*

MURIEL. *(Half to herself.)* God, you are so young …

NORM. Here, why don't you use the glasses? *(Norm removes a pair of 3-D glasses and puts them on her. As Young Muriel watches the screen, Norm watches her, noting her reaction.)*

MURIEL. *(As if cueing him.)* "You like Philip Archer?"

NORM. You like Philip Archer?

YOUNG MURIEL. Oh sure, he's swell.

NORM. You think he's good-looking?

YOUNG MURIEL. I think he's dreamy, don't you?

NORM. I don't know. *(Muriel smiles wistfully and shakes her head.)* You think he's better-looking than me? *(Young Muriel just gives him a "dream on" look.)*

MURIEL. *(Half to herself.)* Not a chance.

NORM. Never mind, I don't want to know. *(They chuckle, then return to watching the movie. Young Muriel glances at Norm, then back at the screen.)*

MURIEL. Go ahead, ask him.

YOUNG MURIEL. You think I'm prettier than Charlotte Ayres? *(Pause. He grins.)*

MURIEL. Tell her.

NORM. You're much prettier than Charlotte Ayres.

YOUNG MURIEL. You're just saying that.

NORM. Much prettier. I mean she's fine, she's pretty, but like I said, she's stuck-up, so that takes something away. But you, you're not stuck-up at all, so … / so that adds something.

MURIEL. *(Simultaneous with Norm.)* "so that adds something," very smooth, Norm. *(Young Muriel eyes him carefully.)*

YOUNG MURIEL. This the way you talk with Hazel?

NORM. Nah, we don't really talk.

YOUNG MURIEL. Then what do you two do up here all the time?

NORM. Why don't you ask her, since you girls are so tight?

YOUNG MURIEL. Maybe I did.

NORM. What did she say?

YOUNG MURIEL.   MURIEL.
A lot of stuff Daddy   "A lot of stuff Daddy
wouldn't want to hear.   wouldn't want to hear."

MURIEL. ... boy, that's the truth. *(Norm and Young Muriel chuckle, embarrassed. Pause.)*

YOUNG MURIEL. We used to play this ... game up here. That our mom taught us.

MURIEL. Oh no ...

NORM. What kind of game?

YOUNG MURIEL. Never mind ...

NORM. No, tell me.

MURIEL. Don't.

YOUNG MURIEL. It's stupid, really.

NORM. Tell me.

MURIEL. Please don't.

YOUNG MURIEL. Well ...

NORM. Go on.

MURIEL. Let it be ours.

YOUNG MURIEL. If you turn out the lights?

MURIEL. Noooo ...

YOUNG MURIEL. And sit next to the projector, and hold your arms out front like this? You can pretend you're flying a plane. *(Muriel makes a sound of disappointment and shakes her head disapprovingly.)*

NORM. Huh. *(Pause.)* Show me what you used to do.

YOUNG MURIEL. No ...   MURIEL. You don't have to ...
(Young Muriel moves away from the viewport.)

NORM. Come on.

YOUNG MURIEL. It's silly.

NORM. No it isn't; show me.

YOUNG MURIEL. We promised.   MURIEL. You promised.

NORM. What do you mean? Promised who?

YOUNG MURIEL. Anyway, it's just a girl thing, that's all.

NORM. I don't care, what'd you do?

MURIEL. He won't understand ...

YOUNG MURIEL. Well ...

MURIEL. ... not like we do.

YOUNG MURIEL. I'd sit here, and Hazel would sit there.

MURIEL. Oh, Muriel. *(To Muriel's astonishment, Young Muriel looks directly at her. She gasps.)*

NORM. On the stool.

YOUNG MURIEL. *(Looking at Muriel.)* Yeah. *(Norm moves the stool into position.)*

NORM. Okay, then what?

YOUNG MURIEL. *(Turning back to Norm.)* I really should go.

NORM. No no, this is cute. Then what?

YOUNG MURIEL. *(Beat.)* Then Hazel —

NORM. Wait, we forgot to turn out the light.

MURIEL. *(Tentatively.)* Muriel? *(As Norm hits the light switch, the lighting instantly becomes stranger yet. Young Muriel turns to look at Muriel, who gasps again.)* Oh God ... *(Pause.)*

YOUNG MURIEL. What.

MURIEL. *(Beat.)* Uhh ... *(Muriel looks back at Norm, who stands motionless in the shadows by the light switch, then back at Young Muriel.)* I ... I don't ...

YOUNG MURIEL. *What. (Pause.)*

MURIEL. In a minute you're going to kiss that boy.

YOUNG MURIEL. *(Beat.)* No I'm not ...

MURIEL. Yes you are.

YOUNG MURIEL. He's Hazel's boyfriend, not mine.

MURIEL. Oh believe me, I know ...

YOUNG MURIEL. Then why / did you —

MURIEL. ... but you didn't come up here to use the bathroom. *(Pause.)* Did you.

YOUNG MURIEL. I just wanted to be up here again.

NORM. There we go.

MURIEL. *(Distracted by him.)* Wha — ?

NORM. *(Taking his seat again.)* Then Hazel what?

YOUNG MURIEL. Then Hazel would say —

NORM. Sit down.

MURIEL. Wait, Muriel ... *(Norm takes Young Muriel's hand and gently pulls her onto the chair in front of him.)*

NORM. What's she say?

YOUNG MURIEL. She says, "Pilot to navigator, come in navigator."

NORM. If she's the pilot, how come she's behind you?

YOUNG MURIEL. Well, these old planes, the pilot sat in the back.
NORM. Oh, yeah. *(He holds his arms out front as if gripping the stick of an airplane.)*
MURIEL. I want you to stop. *(Young Muriel turns toward Muriel.)*
NORM. So then what?
YOUNG MURIEL. *(Facing front.)* Then Hazel says, / "All controls adjusted and trimmed, check."
MURIEL. Did you hear me? I said I want you to stop.
NORM. All controls adjusted and trimmed, check.
MURIEL. Listen ...
YOUNG MURIEL. Ailerons normal / position, check.
MURIEL. Listen to me *listen Muriel! (Muriel takes Young Muriel's face in her hands and turns her head toward her. Norm freezes, arms in place.)* In a minute you're going to kiss that boy.
YOUNG MURIEL. You already said that.
MURIEL. And once you've kissed him, you'll fall in love with him ...
YOUNG MURIEL. No I won't.
MURIEL. ... and once you're in love, you'll marry him.
YOUNG MURIEL. *(Pushing Muriel's hands away.)* You don't have to marry someone just 'cause you kiss him.
MURIEL. Not usually, no ...
YOUNG MURIEL. So.
MURIEL. ... but you will.
YOUNG MURIEL. I won't! I'll just kiss him and walk away. *(Norm rests his forearms on Young Muriel's shoulders. Young Muriel turns her head toward Norm.)*
NORM. My arms got tired. *(Young Muriel faces front again.)*
MURIEL. Go back down.
YOUNG MURIEL. Prime engines.
MURIEL. Please, Muriel.
NORM. Engines primed.
YOUNG MURIEL. Number one and number two mixture rich.
NORM. Check.
MURIEL. Just walk away.
YOUNG MURIEL. Crank engine one.
NORM. *(Leaning forward.)* Check.
MURIEL. *I know you can hear me ...*

65

YOUNG MURIEL. Um ... crank engine two.

NORM. Check.

MURIEL. *(An urgent whisper.)* Go! Now! *(After a beat, Young Muriel stands suddenly, heading towards the stairway, past where Muriel is standing. Muriel follows just behind her, urging her on.)*

YOUNG MURIEL. I ought to go.

NORM. Sorry, I'm sorry ...

YOUNG MURIEL. No ...

NORM. Don't go, please ...

MURIEL. *Go.*

NORM. Come on ... *(Norm reaches out and grabs the hand of Muriel, who watches Young Muriel disappear through the doorway. Registering the touch of Norm's hand, Muriel turns to look at her hand, then looks up at Norm.)* You'll miss the best part.

MURIEL. Uhh ... *(Muriel looks after Young Muriel as Norm begins to pull her back to the "airplane.")*

NORM. Sit down. *(Muriel hesitates.)*

MURIEL. *(Terrified.)* Maybe I shouldn't.

NORM. Why not — you think I got germs?

MURIEL. I — I'm really not supposed to be up here.

NORM. That's bullcrap. Hazel's up here all the time.

MURIEL. Well, she's Hazel.

NORM. Like your old man'll notice while he's fixing a leak in the ladies' lounge. *(Norm pulls Muriel onto the chair in front of him.)* So then what? *(Pause.)*

MURIEL. Then ... Hazel says — *(Pause.)*

NORM. What. *(Beat.)* Hazel says what?

MURIEL. She says — *(Muriel cannot continue. Young Muriel has reappeared in the doorway.)*

YOUNG MURIEL. Go ahead, ask him.

NORM. *(Beat. To Muriel:)* What?

YOUNG MURIEL. *(Beat.)* Go ahead.

MURIEL. *(Beat. Not looking at him:)* Why don't you touch me anymore?

NORM. *(Beat.)* Huh?

MURIEL. Why don't you kiss me?

NORM. *(Beat.)* What are you —

MURIEL. I don't mean a peck on the cheek, "I'm off to Denver, see

66

you in a few days," I mean a *kiss.* What happened to that? *(Pause.)*
YOUNG MURIEL. Go ahead. Ask him. *(Muriel shuts her eyes. Beat. Then she opens her eyes, gets up from the chair, takes a few steps, but is stopped by Young Muriel.)* Ask him.
MURIEL. *(Beat.)* Who's in Denver?
NORM. *(Beat.)* What?
MURIEL. What's her name?
NORM. That's bullcrap.
YOUNG MURIEL. Tell her. *(Pause.)* Tell her. *(Pause. Norm looks away. Pause.)*
MURIEL. *(Quietly.)* What do I do with you? What do I say? Hey, Norm, can we go to the movies tonight? Do you want to buy a movie theater? What do I say? Hmm? Where do we go from here? *(Pause.)*
YOUNG MURIEL. *(To Norm.)* Oh, this part is the best!
MURIEL. *(Turning towards her.)* What?
YOUNG MURIEL. Can you turn it up?
NORM. *(Turning towards her.)* Huh? *(Young Muriel crosses in front of Muriel to take her old position on the chair.)*
YOUNG MURIEL. The big love scene. Can you turn up the sound? *(Norm looks over to Muriel.)*
NORM. Uh … sure. *(Beat. Muriel turns up the sound, but faces away from Norm and Young Muriel, listening, but unable to watch. As before, the tinny sounds of* Wings Over Water *are heard, along with a low airplane hum. Norm leans forward as he and Young Muriel look out the viewport.)*
AMELIA. *(V.O.)* Well, what's past is past. We can't live yesterday over again.
CARL. *(V.O.)* Maybe we can. *(Beat.)* Kiss me, Amelia. Kiss me all the way to yesterday.
AMELIA. *(V.O.)* What difference will it make? If the fuel runs out —
CARL. *(V.O.)* Then let it run out. I love you.
AMELIA. *(V.O.)* Oh, do you really mean it?
CARL. *(V.O.)* I've loved you to the stars, I'll love you to the bottom of the sea … *(Norm kisses Young Muriel, billowed by swelling romantic music. The changeover bell begins ringing. Muriel covers her face with her hand as the sounds and kisses continue. Lights fade to black.)*

Reel Five

In darkness, dialogue from Wings Over Water *plays:*

CARL. *(V.O.)* Why do you fly, Amelia?

AMELIA. *(V.O.)* Surely you're not going to tell me it's a man's job, too?

CARL. *(V.O.)* Don't be silly. You're living proof of that. But why must you always fly farther, faster and higher than any man?

AMELIA. *(V.O.)* I suppose to prove that any woman can.

CARL. *(V.O.)* You're not just any woman.

AMELIA. *(V.O.)* Yes I am, Carl. I'm made of flesh and blood like any woman. As prone to tears and petty jealousies. And just as sentimental as the next girl when I find a dozen roses in my room. But like any woman, I'm tough and stubborn as a mule when I know what it is I want.

CARL. *(V.O.)* Meaning?

AMELIA. *(V.O.)* Meaning if I want to circle the globe, I'll do it. If I want to break a speed record, I'll break it. And if I choose to fly as high as the stars, you'd better learn to read your charts by starlight. Because I won't settle for the moon.

CARL. *(V.O.)* Then I guess I'll learn to read by starlight.

AMELIA. *(V.O.)* Excellent — I was afraid I'd have to go by myself. *(Sound fades as lights come up to normal in the projection room, a few hours later. The first projector is still running, the second is empty. The onstage speaker is silent. Muriel, wearing Hazel's union jacket and 3-D glasses, stands between the two projectors, looking out a viewport. Hazel enters hastily, if a bit unsteadily. She stops upon seeing the moving projector, but does not see Muriel, who is hidden by the projector. As Hazel quickly approaches the running projector, Muriel hears her, looks around, and speaks.)*

MURIEL. Oh, you're back.

HAZEL. *(Startled.)* Jesus! What are you doing here?

MURIEL. Just watching the movie.

HAZEL. With the sound off?

MURIEL. *(Looking out.)* I've been enjoying the quiet. *(Hazel looks at her curiously, then focuses on the moving projector.)*

HAZEL. Who set this up?

MURIEL. I did. *(Hazel gives her a look, then opens the panel and checks out how it has been threaded up.)* How was your dinner?

HAZEL. Sorry I'm late.

MURIEL. Don't worry about it.

HAZEL. Service in that place gets slower every year. By the time we got the check, our waiter needed a shave. How'd it go tonight?

MURIEL. What do you mean?

HAZEL. Back at the house.

MURIEL. Oh. I don't know, I never went.

HAZEL. *(Beat.)* Never *went?*

MURIEL. No, I stayed here.

HAZEL. What about the ... thing? With everybody —

MURIEL. I needed to be alone for a bit.

HAZEL. But you made such a big deal ...

MURIEL. I needed to be alone. *(Pause.)*

HAZEL. Boy, you and I are scoring family points tonight. *(Of film threading:)* This looks all right ...

MURIEL. How'd things go with you and Ray? *(Beat. Hazel leans her head wearily against the projector.)*

HAZEL. Great.

MURIEL. Then you got what you wanted?

HAZEL. You could say that.

MURIEL. Oh, Hazel. Well. I'm happy for you.

HAZEL. I got more than I asked for. *(Hazel begins fanning herself.)*

MURIEL. What are you talking about?

HAZEL. It's a mad mad mad mad world ... *(Hazel glances out the viewport.)*

MURIEL. What happened?

HAZEL. Why are you showing this?

MURIEL. What?

HAZEL. Tonight's supposed to be *Casablanca.*

MURIEL. I know ...

HAZEL. Then why —

MURIEL. I needed to see this one last time. *(Hazel looks at her.)*

69

HAZEL. *(Beat.)* And nobody said anything?

MURIEL. Not to me.

HAZEL. Huh. Maybe they're so old, they'll never notice.

MURIEL. *What happened? (Pause.)*

HAZEL. I'm getting back together with Ray.

MURIEL. *(Beat. Quietly:)* Oh thank God.

HAZEL. Stupid, isn't it? Oh, Muriel … I was so ready for him to lie, cheat, bully, threaten — anything to get what he wanted. Hell, it's what I was gonna do. And first thing he does — first thing out of his mouth — he *apologizes.* I could have killed him.

MURIEL. Then he's coming back?

HAZEL. Soon as the semester's over. He wants me to join him in Berkeley till then. Oh, God, I'm so happy. I'm so ashamed.

MURIEL. Cut it out …

HAZEL. For being weak.

MURIEL. You're not weak.

HAZEL. People always think I'm so strong.

MURIEL. You are.

HAZEL. No I'm not. I'm just … loud. If I were strong, I'd have spat in his face and stayed single and miserable for life. *(She fans herself and looks around the room.)* What a dump. *(She begins gathering up her clothes and other items.)*

MURIEL. I was praying you two would get back together.

HAZEL. Oh shut up.

MURIEL. I was. You were made for each other.

HAZEL. Yeah, well, Ray says the good lord brought us together to spare two other people. Is it hot in here, or is it me? *(Hazel continues to pick up.)*

MURIEL. Listen, I need to tell you something …

HAZEL. Sure, go ahead. *(But she has entered the bathroom.)*

MURIEL. What are you doing?

HAZEL. *(Off.)* Picking up. This place is a mess.

MURIEL. You don't have to do that tonight.

HAZEL. *(Off.)* Yes I do. I'm sick of this airless, squalid little room. *(Hazel reenters, fanning herself.)* Christ, I think I'm having a hot flash; I thought I was done with those. *(Hazel picks up a box of Trivial Pursuit question cards in her other hand.)* There's a bottle of vodka in a shoebox on the floor of the closet. Keep it or ditch it, whatever you want.

MURIEL. You're not leaving tonight, are you?

HAZEL. First thing tomorrow; Dad's affairs can wait. Also one in the ceiling of the stairway. *(Hazel looks around the table for the box top.)*

MURIEL. You really shouldn't drink so much, you know.

HAZEL. *I know,* I'm a codependent alcoholic, but I say screw it; if you're gonna be codependent you might as well do it with somebody else. And if you also happen to be alcoholic, at least you're not drinking alone. Where's the top to this?

MURIEL. On the bottom. *(Hazel turns the box over, spilling all the cards onto the floor.)*

HAZEL. Oh, Christ ...

MURIEL. Here, I'll get it.

HAZEL. I'm sorry ...

MURIEL. Don't worry about it.

HAZEL. *(Stopping her.)* I mean it: I'm. Sorry.

MURIEL. Don't be silly. It's just a couple cards.

HAZEL. Not for that; for being such a bitchy broad.

MURIEL. You're not a bitchy broad.

HAZEL. Oh, come on — thirty-one years?

MURIEL. All right, sometimes you can be a bitchy broad.

HAZEL. And for saying shitty things about you, and Norm.

MURIEL. That's all right.

HAZEL. I didn't mean them.

MURIEL. Yes you did.

HAZEL. I did, but I was bitter back then.

MURIEL. Listen:

HAZEL. I think you and Norm are great together ...

MURIEL. I'm leaving him.

HAZEL. ... and if you two wanna fix up this — *WHAT?*

MURIEL. I'm leaving him.

HAZEL. Oh my God ...

MURIEL. Not yet, not ...

HAZEL. No ...

MURIEL. ... officially. I called to tell him to pick me up here, and that we needed to talk.

HAZEL. Then you still have time to change your mind ...

MURIEL. I won't.

HAZEL. Think it over ...

MURIEL. I have.

HAZEL. Maybe sleep on it, just in case you're wrong ...

MURIEL. I'm not.

HAZEL. *I* was wrong.

MURIEL. I'm not.

HAZEL. *(Beat.)* Oh, God. Oh, God, I feel awful. I'm sick about this. After I made all those bald jokes ...

MURIEL. This has nothing to do with you.

HAZEL. You seem so calm about it; have you been drinking?

MURIEL. No.

HAZEL. Maybe you should be. *(Hazel exits into the bathroom. Muriel looks out the viewport. From the bathroom, the sound of porcelain rattling on porcelain.)*

MURIEL. I'd give anything to have that kiss back, Hazel. The first one. Then walk away. If I could do it over, that's what I'd do. *(Hazel emerges from the bathroom with a bottle and glass of vodka. She holds the glass out to Muriel.)*

HAZEL. Here — I wish it were the good stuff ...

MURIEL. Oh no, thanks, I'm fine.

HAZEL. Come on, take it. It'll calm my nerves. *(Muriel takes it, then looks out the viewport again.)*

MURIEL. As terrible as this may sound, it never really got any better than that — with the music swelling, and that little bell ringing and ringing ... *(Hazel sits on the floor.)*

HAZEL. Whoever designed this floor didn't drink. *(Hazel starts picking up Trivial Pursuit question cards.)*

MURIEL. Here it was only saying, "Wake up ... wake up ... wake up ... " *(Muriel looks around the room.)*

HAZEL. *(Reading a Trivial Pursuit card.)* "Are barnacles plants or animals?"

MURIEL. *(Not looking at her.)* What?

HAZEL. I don't know; who cares? *(She tosses the card away. Muriel places her hand on the projector like an old friend as Hazel reads another card.)* "What can't you stop moving if you suffer from athetosis?"

MURIEL. Hazel ...

HAZEL. Who cares? *(She tosses it away.)*

MURIEL. What are you doing?

HAZEL. *(Reading another.)* "Who did Clifton Webb portray in *Stars and Stripes Forever?*

MURIEL. Hazel?

HAZEL. *(Reading the flip side of the card.)* "John Phillip Sousa." *(She tosses the card away.)*

MURIEL. *(Moving to her.)* Let's fly.

HAZEL. *(Reading another answer.)* "The Crimean War." *(She tosses it away.)*

MURIEL. Please?

HAZEL. *(Reading another answer.)* "Rounders."

MURIEL. One last time.

HAZEL. *(Another.)* "*My Mother the Car.*" *(She tosses it away.)*

MURIEL. Did you hear me?

HAZEL. Why do we bother to remember this shit? These tiny bits of flotsam and jetsam that nobody cares about anymore?

MURIEL. Then let's remember something we do care about. *(Muriel shuts off the overhead lights; Hazel looks at her.)* Get in the plane.

HAZEL. No, Muriel.

MURIEL. Come on.

HAZEL. We're not little girls anymore.

MURIEL. Yes we are.

HAZEL. In case you hadn't noticed, we're both menopausal.

MURIEL. Inside, Hazel — we're as young as we feel. *(She takes Hazel by the arm.)*

HAZEL. Well tonight I feel about a hundred.

MURIEL. Sit down. *(Muriel leads Hazel to the chair.)*

HAZEL. I gotta get home to Ray.

MURIEL. Now close your eyes.

HAZEL. Wait a second …

MURIEL. Close.

HAZEL. *(Standing.)* That's my stool.

MURIEL. I'm the pilot.

HAZEL. Oh, no you don't, the oldest —

MURIEL. This time I'm the pilot.

HAZEL. *(Beat.)* Fair enough. *(Hazel sits.)*

MURIEL. Why you made me navigator, I'll never know. I get lost in the supermarket. *(Muriel sits, shutting her eyes. She takes a deep breath, then:)* "Pilot to navigator, come in navigator … " *(Pause.)* "Pilot to navigator, / come in — "

HAZEL. *(Shutting her eyes.)* "Navigator here."

MURIEL. "Prepare for night flight." *(Lights shift very gradually, recreating the sense of the flying game of years gone by.)* "All electric power off, radio off."

HAZEL. "All electric power off, radio off."

MURIEL. "All controls adjusted and trimmed."

HAZEL. "Check. Ailerons normal position."

MURIEL. "Check. Elevators normal position."

HAZEL. "Check."

MURIEL. "Prime engines."

HAZEL. "Number one and number two mixture rich."

MURIEL. "Crank engine one."

HAZEL. "Engine one cranked."

MURIEL. "Crank engine two."

HAZEL. "Engine two cranked." *(Faintly, the sound of engines, growing gradually louder.)*

MURIEL. "Advance down runway." *(Engine sounds increase. Muriel and Hazel lean back as the "airspeed" increases. After a few seconds:)* "Where shall we go tonight?" *(Hazel opens her eyes slowly. Pause.)* "Where shall we go tonight?" *(Hazel looks out the viewport and down.)* Hazel?

HAZEL. *(Half to herself.)* Son of a bitch … *(Muriel opens her eyes.)*

MURIEL. What's the matter?

HAZEL. It's empty.

MURIEL. Oh.

HAZEL. The theater. There's nobody out there.

MURIEL. I know. *(Hazel turns to look at her.)* I sent them away. *(After a beat, Mike bounds in, out of uniform. He carries a bag of popcorn.)*

MIKE. Hey, why didn't you tell me?

HAZEL. *(To Muriel.)* Sent them away? *(Muriel nods.)*

MIKE. I just found out across the street.

HAZEL. Found out what?

MIKE. About the theater.

HAZEL. *(To Muriel.)* What about it?

MURIEL. I should have told you sooner.

MIKE. You mean you don't know?

HAZEL. *What are you talking about? (Pause. Mike looks from one to the other.)*

MIKE. Mr. Papadopoulos bought us out. *(Long pause.)*

HAZEL. *(To Muriel.)* What do you mean he bought us out?

MURIEL. Apparently Daddy sold him the theater three weeks ago. He's just waiting for settlement to move the whole video store over here. *(Hazel, stunned, can only sit.)*

MIKE. I figured you knew. *(Pause.)* Sorry. *(Beat.)* My friends were all psyched to see *Casablanca* tonight. They heard it was pretty cool. *(Beat.)* But I guess they can always get it across the street.

MURIEL. *(Watching Hazel carefully.)* Oh, I'm sure. *(Pause. Mike fills in the uncomfortable dead air.)*

MIKE. Brenda says Mr. Papadopoulos is gonna tear out all the seats and level the floor in the next two months. Really get things going for spring.

MURIEL. Is that right. *(Hazel begins laughing quietly to herself.)*

MIKE. Gonna be the biggest in Philly. *(Beat.)* He's even gonna make her assistant manager — which is great, 'cause that means she'll, you know, stick around. *(Mike notices the mess on the floor.)* What happened to all the cards? *(Mike sets the popcorn down and begins collecting and reordering the Trivial Pursuit cards. Long pause. Hazel wipes her eyes.)*

HAZEL. Well. Looks like the Old Man pulled another fast one …

MURIEL. Yeah. Looks like. *(Pause.)*

HAZEL. At least we'll never have to brush those damn seats again. *(Muriel looks at her and smiles. Pause. Mike unobtrusively continues picking up cards.)* He looked so small this afternoon, in that great big box. *(Beat.)* Who'd ever think he could rant and rage, and drive his wife and daughters to the farthest room … *(Pause.)* What'll you do?

MURIEL. What do you mean?

HAZEL. With your life. You've gotta do something.

MURIEL. Oh … I don't know. *(Beat.)* Maybe I'll go to college. *(Hazel gives her a look.)* Bryn Mawr took me once.

HAZEL. I've heard of deferred admission, but still …

MIKE. I just got a job at the video store.

HAZEL. I'm not worried about you.

MIKE. No, I just meant Mrs. Palmer could maybe get one, too.
'Cause they're expanding and everything.
MURIEL. I don't think so, Mike, but thanks.
MIKE. No biggie. *(Pause. Hazel considers Muriel.)*
HAZEL. You okay for tonight?
MURIEL. I'm fine; go home to Ray. I'll talk to Norm and the
girls at the hotel, then come back to the house.
MIKE. *Oh* — Mrs. Palmer?
MURIEL. Yeah?
MIKE. I forgot. Your husband's here.
HAZEL. *(Beat.)* Downstairs?
MIKE. Outside. He said he'd wait in the car.
HAZEL. *(Beat.)* I'll tell him you're on your way. You take your time.
MURIEL. Thanks.
HAZEL. We'll figure this all out. *(After a moment's hesitation, Hazel
gives Muriel a big hug, then turns to Mike.)* "Here's lookin' at you,
kid." *(She hugs him, hard.)* Don't grow up to be an asshole, okay?
MIKE. Okay. *(Hazel exits with her belongings. Mike watches as
Muriel wipes a tear from her cheek. After a moment, he extends the
popcorn to her, a gesture of consolation.)* Want some popcorn?
MURIEL. Hm? Oh — no thanks. I don't eat popcorn.
MIKE. How come?
MURIEL. It's … a long story. *(Mike nods vaguely. Pause.)*
MIKE. You can borrow my game if you want. *(Muriel just turns
and looks at him.)* Since your family's in town and all.
MURIEL. I don't think so, Mike, but thanks.
MIKE. No biggie. *(Pause.)* I knew this thing with the theater was
gonna happen. Even before I heard anything.
MURIEL. How?
MIKE. I just knew it. You look at all the tons of people over there
in the video store, then you look at the couple people here, and it
totally makes sense. It was just a matter of time. Like, when I was
a kid? Everybody thought eight-tracks were so great. Everybody
had to have an eight-track; we even had one. Now everybody
knows eight-tracks were stupid.
MURIEL. *(Affectionately patting a projector.)* Well, we're all obso-
lete sometime.
MIKE. Now, if I had a lot of money? I'd put it in VHD.

76

MURIEL. VHD?

MIKE. Video discs. It's like a record, but it's movies.

MURIEL. I'll take your word for it.

MIKE. By 1986, everybody's gonna have VHD. My dad just got a VHD. My mom doesn't even want a VCR. She says she'd rather just go to the movies. But as soon as I make enough, I'm gonna get a VHD. *(Beat. Muriel has been looking intently at Mike.)*

MURIEL. Mike?

MIKE. Huh? *(Pause.)*

MURIEL. Never mind. *(Mike nods vaguely.)*

MIKE. *(Beat.)* Weird thing is, my mom's the one who wanted the eight-track in the first place; now she's afraid if we get a VHD —

MURIEL. Mike.

MIKE. Yeah?

MURIEL. *(Beat.)* Would you kiss me?

MIKE. What do you mean?

MURIEL. I want you to kiss me.

MIKE. *(Beat.)* You mean … *kiss* kiss?

MURIEL. Yeah.

MIKE. *(Beat.)* I already have a girlfriend.

MURIEL. I don't want to be your girlfriend, I just want you to kiss me.

MIKE. *(Beat.)* Isn't that, like, kinda weird?

MURIEL. I don't know. Does it matter? *(Pause. Mike is uncertain.)* Look, I'm never going to tell a soul, and Brenda never needs to know. Just one kiss; then I'll walk away. *(Pause. Mike shrugs.)*

MIKE. Okay. *(Mike moves toward her.)*

MURIEL. Get rid of your gum first. *(Mike removes his gum and throws it in the trash, though he still holds onto the question cards. They kiss for a few seconds. Muriel breaks the kiss.)* Thank you.

MIKE. No biggie.

MURIEL. That was very nice.

MIKE. *(Self-conscious.)* Yeah.

MURIEL. *(Beat.)* Well, I guess I better get downstairs. *(She grabs her belongings.)* Can you lock up?

MIKE. Sure.

MURIEL. You might want to watch the rest of this. *(She hands him her 3-D glasses.)* The ending's wonderful.

MIKE. Okay. *(He takes them. Muriel starts out, then turns back.)*
MURIEL. Oh, and by the way … you were thinking of Clara Barton.
MIKE. Who?
MURIEL. The Civil War nurse was Clara Barton.
MIKE. Oh. Who's Amelia Earhart? *(Pause.)*
MURIEL. Somebody else. *(Mike nods vaguely. Muriel smiles, then exits. Mike looks out the viewport and puts on the 3-D glasses. Lights fade.)*

End of Play

WINGS OVER WATER

[Note: Wings Over Water *is a fictional film. The following two excerpts should, when recorded, evoke the feel of an authentic film from the early 1950s.]*

Excerpt #1

(Plays underneath the dialogue on pages 28–29.)

In the distance, music plays.

CARL. I thought I might find you here.

AMELIA. I wanted to check the left aileron one last time. It's been giving me trouble.

CARL. You'll miss the party.

AMELIA. There'll be plenty of parties if we make it back to the States.

CARL. You mean *when* we get back, don't you?

AMELIA. Of course, that's what I said. Here, hold this for me while I tighten it, will you? *(Pause.)*

CARL. That photographer from New York was trying to find you.

AMELIA. Oh really.

CARL. Wanted to get some shots of you with the locals.

AMELIA. What did you tell him?

CARL. I said you had a headache and went back to the hotel.

AMELIA. Good for you. I see I've taught you a few things about handling the press.

CARL. You've taught me more than a few things. *(Pause.)*

AMELIA. There, that should do it. We've got eighteen hours in the air ahead of us. Might as well not take any chances. *(Pause.)* Why are you looking at me like that?

CARL. Why do you do it?

AMELIA. What do you mean?

CARL. Why do you fly, Amelia?

AMELIA. Surely you're not going to tell me it's a man's job, too?

CARL. Don't be silly. You're living proof of that. But why must you always fly farther, faster and higher than any man?

AMELIA. I suppose to prove that any woman can.

CARL. You're not just any woman.

AMELIA. Yes I am, Carl. I'm made of flesh and blood like any woman. As prone to tears and petty jealousies. And just as sentimental as the next girl when I find a dozen roses in my room. But like any woman, I'm tough and stubborn as a mule when I know what it is I want.

CARL. Meaning?

AMELIA. Meaning if I want to circle the globe, I'll do it. If I want to break a speed record, I'll break it. And if I choose to fly as high as the stars, you'd better learn to read your charts by starlight. Because I won't settle for the moon.

CARL. Then I guess I'll learn to read by starlight.

AMELIA. Excellent — I was afraid I'd have to go by myself.

SAHJI. Miss Air-har! Miss Air-har!

AMELIA. Oh — hello, Sahji. What's that you've got there?

SAHJI. The children from the village — we make you a present for the pretty lady flyer.

AMELIA. Why thank you, Sahji — it's beautiful. May I put it on?

SAHJI. Yes, please, Miss Air-har. I pick the flowers myself.

AMELIA. Then I'll treasure it always.

SAHJI. You come to the party, yes?

AMELIA. Yes, I promise.

SAHJI. Soon?

AMELIA. Yes, very soon. I'll just be a moment.

SAHJI. Okay, goo-bye. *(Pause.)*

CARL. I see you're breaking new ground in headgear as well as aviation.

AMELIA. Do I look thoroughly silly?

CARL. No, you're very fetching. *(Beat.)* These children love you.

AMELIA. Well, they're children.

CARL. No, it's not that. You'll notice they don't bring me crowns of flowers.

AMELIA. Would you like to wear mine?

CARL. You're special to them. Not just the children, not just New Guinea, but everywhere. People around the world buy newspapers just to read your name, watch newsreels to see your face and hear of your latest adventure. They love you, Amelia.

AMELIA. I'm not so sure I'd call that love. Curiosity, perhaps.

CARL. It's more than that. Much more. *(Pause.)* I appreciate what you said earlier.

AMELIA. About what?

CARL. About your being a woman. *(Beat.)* So often on this trip, with all the preparations, we only have time to act as professionals — navigator, pilot ... As if that's all that mattered.

AMELIA. Isn't it?

CARL. Is it? Or is there — could there be something else?

AMELIA. *(Beat.)* I think we'd better get back to the party ...

CARL. No, listen. If we go back to that party, we'll never say what needs to be said.

AMELIA. Carl ...

CARL. I know what you're thinking: "Carl's had too much of that strong native drink ... "

AMELIA. That's not what I'm thinking.

CARL. Well maybe I have. That doesn't mean what I'm saying isn't true. I just never had the courage to say it.

AMELIA. Perhaps some things are best left unsaid.

CARL. No ...

SAHJI. Miss Air-har, Miss Air-har! Come quick!

AMELIA. Yes, Sahji?

SAHJI. My father send for you so you can cut the pig.

AMELIA. The pig?

SAHJI. It's ready to be eat.

AMELIA. Oh. All right.

SAHJI. He ask the American man to come, too.

AMELIA. *(Beat.)* Carl?

CARL. I suppose that's me. Well, wouldn't want to disappoint. Let's go cut up a pig, shall we?

81

WINGS OVER WATER

Excerpt #2

(Plays underneath the dialogue on pages 33–35.)

The sound of a low airplane hum.

CARL. Why don't you try the radio again?

AMELIA. I've tried and tried, but there's no response.

CARL. Then try again, it's our only hope.

AMELIA. KHAQQ calling Itasca. We must be on you but cannot see you … Gas is running low. Been unable to reach you by radio. We are flying at altitude 1000 feet, over. *(Beat.)* When you took our bearings through the clouds, are you sure you caught the North Star?

CARL. My sextant doesn't lie. *(Suddenly, the airplane hum begins to sputter and the movie music turns dramatic. After a few moments, the engine hum returns to normal, as does the music.)*

AMELIA. We're down to the reserve tank. Twelve gallons, that's all.

CARL. That gives us less than twenty minutes. *(Pause.)* Aren't you frightened?

AMELIA. I'd been trying not to notice.

CARL. Well I'm frightened. Flying on fumes, a thousand feet above the largest, deepest ocean in the world … You'd have to be a hero or a fool not to be frightened.

AMELIA. Which am I?

CARL. *(Beat.)* You're no fool, Amelia … *(The music turns romantic.)* Last night, in the hangar, the way you looked … those flowers that native boy placed in your hair …

AMELIA. Please, Carl, not now.

CARL. You were waiting for me to kiss you, weren't you? *(Beat.)* Well, I wanted to kiss you; I should have kissed you, only …

AMELIA. Only what?

CARL. You know what; we both know.

AMELIA. Well, what's past is past. We can't live yesterday over again.

CARL. Maybe we can. *(Beat.)* According to the chronometer, in two minutes, we'll cross the 180th parallel.

AMELIA. The International Date Line ...

CARL. That's right. On this side it's Monday, but over there it's Sunday — the day we left New Guinea, the day we should have kissed but didn't.

AMELIA. Oh, Carl ...

CARL. Kiss me, Amelia. Kiss me all the way to yesterday.

AMELIA. What difference will it make? If the fuel runs out —

CARL. Then let it run out. I love you.

AMELIA. Oh, do you really mean it?

CARL. I've loved you to the stars, I'll love you to the bottom of the sea ... *(The music swells and plays through the end of Reel Two.)*

PROPERTY LIST

Trivial Pursuit game
Cigarette and lighter/matches
3-D glasses
Bag of popcorn
Watch (HAZEL, MURIEL)
Projector reel (HAZEL, MURIEL)
Can of beer (HAZEL)
Film cans (HAZEL, MURIEL)
Paperback book (NORM)
Handbag/purse (MURIEL, HAZEL)
Leather flying helmet (MURIEL)
Video boxes (BRENDA)
Jacket (MURIEL)
Eyeglasses (MURIEL)
Drinking glass (HAZEL)
Dress on hanger (HAZEL)
Vodka bottle (HAZEL)
Folded document (HAZEL)
Photograph (HAZEL)
Clothes (HAZEL)
Chewing gum (MIKE)

SOUND EFFECTS

Voice-over of two little girls
Bell
Voice-over of two little girls and mother
Voice-over film excerpts (one man, one woman, one child)
Back of a toilet being lifted and replaced
Toilet flushing
Buzz of a telephone
Airplane engine

NEW PLAYS

★ **HONOUR by Joanna Murray-Smith.** In a series of intense confrontations, a wife, husband, lover and daughter negotiate the forces of passion, history, responsibility and honour. "HONOUR makes for surprisingly interesting viewing. Tight, crackling dialogue (usually played out in punchy verbal duels) captures characters unable to deal with emotions ... Murray-Smith effectively places her characters in situations that strip away pretense." –*Variety* "... the play's virtues are strong: a distinctive theatrical voice, passionate concerns ... HONOUR might just capture a few honors of its own." –*Time Out Magazine* [1M, 3W] ISBN: 0-8222-1683-3

★ **MR. PETERS' CONNECTIONS by Arthur Miller.** Mr. Miller describes the protagonist as existing in a dream-like state when the mind is "freed to roam from real memories to conjectures, from trivialities to tragic insights, from terror of death to glorying in one's being alive." With this memory play, the Tony Award and Pulitzer Prize-winner reaffirms his stature as the world's foremost dramatist. "... a cross between Joycean stream-of-consciousness and Strindberg's dream plays, sweetened with a dose of William Saroyan's philosophical whimsy ... CONNECTIONS is most intriguing ..." –*The NY Times* [5M, 3W] ISBN: 0-8222-1687-6

★ **THE WAITING ROOM by Lisa Loomer.** Three women from different centuries meet in a doctor's waiting room in this dark comedy about the timeless quest for beauty – and its cost. "... THE WAITING ROOM ... is a bold, risky melange of conflicting elements that is ... terrifically moving ... There's no resisting the fierce emotional pull of the play." –*The NY Times* "... one of the high points of this year's Off-Broadway season ... THE WAITING ROOM is well worth a visit." –*Back Stage* [7M, 4W, flexible casting] ISBN: 0-8222-1594-2

★ **THE OLD SETTLER by John Henry Redwood.** A sweet-natured comedy about two church-going sisters in 1943 Harlem and the handsome young man who rents a room in their apartment. "For all of its decent sentiments, THE OLD SETTLER avoids sentimentality. It has the authenticity and lack of pretense of an Early American sampler." –*The NY Times* "We've had some fine plays Off-Broadway this season, and this is one of the best." –*The NY Post* [1M, 3W] ISBN: 0-8-222-1642-6

★ **LAST TRAIN TO NIBROC by Arlene Hutton.** In 1940 two young strangers share a seat on a train bound east only to find their paths will cross again. "All aboard. LAST TRAIN TO NIBROC is a sweetly told little chamber romance." –*Show Business* "... [a] gently charming little play, reminiscent of Thornton Wilder in its look at rustic Americans who are to be treasured for their simplicity and directness ..." –*Associated Press* "The old formula of boy wins girls, boy loses girl, boy wins girl still works ... [a] well-made play that perfectly captures a slice of small-town-life-gone-by." –*Back Stage* [1M, 1W] ISBN: 0-8222-1753-8

★ **OVER THE RIVER AND THROUGH THE WOODS by Joe DiPietro.** Nick sees both sets of his grandparents every Sunday for dinner. This is routine until he has to tell them that he's been offered a dream job in Seattle. The news doesn't sit so well. "A hilarious family comedy that is even funnier than his long running musical revue *I Love You, You're Perfect, Now Change*." –*Back Stage* "Loaded with laughs every step of the way." –*Star-Ledger* [3M, 3W] ISBN: 0-8222-1712-0

★ **SIDE MAN by Warren Leight.** 1999 Tony Award winner. This is the story of a broken family and the decline of jazz as popular entertainment. "... a tender, deeply personal memory play about the turmoil in the family of a jazz musician as his career crumbles at the dawn of the age of rock-and-roll ..." –*The NY Times* "[SIDE MAN] is an elegy for two things – a lost world and a lost love. When the two notes sound together in harmony, it is moving and graceful ..." –*The NY Daily News* "An atmospheric memory play ... with crisp dialogue and clearly drawn characters ... reflects the passing of an era with persuasive insight ... The joy and despair of the musicians is skillfully illustrated." –*Variety* [5M, 3W] ISBN: 0-8222-1721-X

DRAMATISTS PLAY SERVICE, INC.
440 Park Avenue South, New York, NY 10016 212-683-8960 Fax 212-213-1539
postmaster@dramatists.com   www.dramatists.com